THE CAT SECRET

SYLVIE STERLING

DEDICATION

This book is dedicated to my cat companion **Lennie**. He was my best friend and my soulmate, and when he crossed over in 2022, he left a huge gap in my life. But I also know that his passing spiraled another leap of moving forward in my life.

My dearest Lennie, I am counting the days for you to come back to me, and I love you infinitely. In much gratitude and love,

 Sylvie

CONTENTS

PREFACE

This book was on the drawing board for almost 7 years. I had the idea for the book title when I went through my first spiritual awakening, and I started many attempts to write it. But it wasn't flowing. I trashed one manuscript after the other and kept going back to zero point. Eventually, I stopped writing altogether.

I often wondered why it took me so long to write my heart project. Now, with hindsight, I understand: I've grown so much in these past 7 years, that it would have been a very different book back then. But it needed to come through me just the way it is now: effortlessly, in one go, and not premeditated. The content of this book is of a higher vibration and will give you light codes and activations as you are reading it.

How did the book come about, after all? I surrendered. I surrendered it to the Universe and to my higher self. I said if I was truly meant to write this book, with this title and this content, then it'll come about, one way or another.

And then the most beautiful thing happened: I opened my laptop and put my fingers on the keyboard. The collective consciousness of cats came in, and they started to channel the book for me! What had taken me 7 long years of thinking, and planning, and attempting to write, now came flowing through me effortlessly, as my fingers were flying across the keyboard and my mind was in floating mode. The cat collective and my higher guidance took over the process and channeled the book for me. Its entire content came through me within a short window of only 4 weeks, and its deep wisdom surprised me at times as much as it might surprise you.

One thing I can promise: you are in for a treat, dear cat lover. After reading this book, you'll never look at your cat the same way again. You'll have a much deeper connection and higher understanding of what your cat is in your life for, and how you can live a happy and purposeful life together. With that, I am handing the spotlight over to the cat collective. With love and awe,

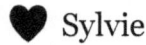 Sylvie

1

WHAT IS THE CAT SECRET

This is not your ordinary cat book. This book will take you on an extraordinary journey – not only of understanding cats – but also of self-exploration, wisdom, and deep insights, presented from your cat's perspective and the cat collective, and also from the elders and the ones that came here to Earth before you remember.

It is going to be an exploration of yourself and the highest realms of joy and love. You'll be taken into your own deep wealth of wisdom and you'll be called to remember how to fulfill your soul's purpose.

So let's dive right into the matter of the subject of this book: **PURPOSE.**

The cat secret is as old as the human journey on this planet. All we ever wonder about is: why am I here? What is the purpose of my life? Well, it's much the same for every human and animal on the planet: you are here on a mission. You are here to contribute to the whole, to this experience you call Earth. You are here with a divine mission and with a deep purpose. And so is your cat.

Thus, the cat secret is very simple: PURPOSE.

It's about their purpose, and yours! For your cat's purpose is to help you with your purpose.

The cats are not here on Earth to just sit still and do nothing. They are here to experience the world with all their senses. They are here to explore, and to feel, see, hear, touch, and sense everything around them. Just watch a cat outdoors, stalking a butterfly or touching an unknown object with their paws. They will do so with undivided attention to the here and now, and to explore this world in all its facets, colors, smells, scents, and haptic experiences.

This is also true for humans. You came here to do something important: to create a new world. Every day you get up, you create. You see the world with your own special eyes. You feel and hear things, you haptically touch the world around you, and then you go and create and contribute to the world every single day.

Yes, we are talking about the secret to life itself: creation. Purposeful creation. You are here to create! You are here to walk, breathe, and create a magical, wondrous world for yourself and others. This is the purpose and the reason for you being here. In the physical, it's especially challenging – but oh so rewarding – to create something out of nothing.

Look back at your life and take in all the magical and great things you have created for yourself. Look at your home, your family, and your animal companions. Look at your work endeavors, and what you have created there. What is it that you are most proud of? And what is it that you wish you could change or do differently? Now is the time to do so.

As you set out every morning, on each new day, you create, create, create your world – with your thoughts, your feelings, and your emotions. These then create your actions, which then turn into things – be they physical or in the ether. But you continue to create, create, create. That is what you are here for. That is the divine plan behind your existence. You came into the physical to create a new world!

So the grand divine plan is part of your creation, or better your creation is a part of the grand divine plan.

Where is this information coming from? Let's introduce the Collective, a group of non-physical beings that helped channel this book. They are here to help you ease into a place of joy and effortless creation. It's what life is all about: being effortless, being in your heart, and feeling your joy.

This book is all about love and life – and about the secrets of the most beloved animal on the planet: the cat.

The cats are channeling a very large part of this book, with the group called the Collective coming in for the higher wisdom.

Before we delve deeper into these subject matters, let us clarify a few concepts and terms that are part of this book, to make it easier to read and understand where this information is coming from.

What is the cat collective?

The cats on this planet, much like the humans on this planet, are all connected in an invisible field of consciousness, just as every species, every living being on this planet, be it humans, animals, plants, or crystals, are all connected and interwoven by a field of light and information. This makes it possible for the cats on this planet to act and communicate as one. The information in this book has largely been channeled by the collective consciousness of cats, which passed on this information by means of speaking through some of their peers in a telepathic way and offering the information to the author of this book who unconsciously received it through typing while being connected to the cat collective stream of consciousness.

What is channeled information?

Channeling is the art of putting your own conscious thoughts aside and letting the information given by another stream of consciousness (in this case the cats and the Collective) come through you by means of writing or speaking. This book has been entirely channeled to the author, who afterward edited the content in a more conscious way to give it her own mark and make it understandable and palpable to her human readers. However, its content was entirely unpremeditated and sometimes surprised the author as much as it might surprise you, the reader, in its depth and wealth of information.

Who is the Collective?

We are a group of non-physical beings in a higher dimensional form, to share wisdom that is beyond the veil so that humanity can tap into this higher knowledge, and wake up to their grandness and uniqueness while increasing their vibrational frequency. We are non- corporeal, but some of us have been where you are, and then have moved into higher realms. We are your guardians, your guides, and your spiritual assistants, if you will. We are here with the purpose of helping you explore your world and your consciousness, and to create your life the way you have laid it out in your soul plan before you incarnated.

So we'll be guiding you through the journey of this book, together with the cats of this world who channeled a large part of the book. Why are we working together on this endeavor?

The Collective are partially feline in nature, or what you would consider feline-human hybrids. You can also call us cat people. We are bringing you this information to also wake you up to your feline nature, as the human race, and to your ties to the feline archetype. We are here to remind you where you are coming from.

The feline archetype is as old as the creation of the universe, and the feline form has been induced in much of what humanity is like – in your genome, your mentality, and your beingness as a species. Upfront, we want to introduce you to the fact that you, dear reader, are more feline in nature than you might think, and that is the reason why you are drawn to this book and to your feline companions in this lifetime.

So what is this book about?

- It's about your deep connection with cats.
- It's about the important purr-pose of cats.
- It's about how cats help you with *YOUR* purpose.
- It's about purposeful living.
- It's about purposeful creation.
- It's about being *YOU*, which is your purpose.
- It's about the purpose of life, which is creation.

But before we go deeper into this, we'll hand it over to our feline friends, the cats of planet Earth, and let them tell the story of how it all began, and how they first started to bond with their human counterparts.

2

THE BOND BETWEEN CATS AND HUMANS

Many of you have wondered what cats really feel or what they are here to do in your life. We, the cats, want to shed light on this endeavor of living together with humans. We have come to stay with you – humans – many eons ago, or more specifically for this planet and for your civilization, we came to stay with you voluntarily about 10,000 years ago, when humans made their transition from being nomads to settling down and beginning farming and agriculture.

We came to you because of necessity... or because of laziness. We saw that many rodents nested around your settlements. We, at the time, were more instinctual than we are now, so we followed the food. We started to hang out around human settlements to get the food source – mice and other small rodents. We would hunt in your grain chambers and storage rooms. We would then get friendly with the big mammals, the owners of the storage containers. As you humans saw that we kept the mice and other rodents away from your precious cargo – corn and other grains – you started to see how gracious we were. How very beautiful we were. How we were helping you keep your food source safe. And that's how the relationship between humans and cats started in this segment of your time.

We started to hang out around you more and more often. You gave us water to drink and shared some of your milk or meals with us. We would come into your dwellings in the winter and the colder months, and you would start to put out a fur bed for us. We would sit by your warm hearth, and soon you realized how our purring and our presence filled your home with light and a feeling of warmth.

You started giving us names, and we graciously accepted all of your hospitality and your care. We became closer and closer, and eventually, we would sit on your lap, sleep in your bed, purr for you, and heal your ailments, both physically and emotionally. We started to become true friends.

Cats seem to have magical powers

The closer our bond grew, the more people became aware of our special powers: to help you get through the winter and to help keep your food safe – yes, that was obvious. But they realized it was much more than that. We seemed to have a quite magical ability around us: to provide a safe space for you to be you – to do your work, whatever that was at the time. To provide love, joy, and a peaceful and healing environment in your home.

Throughout the ages, we've been first feared and then revered, then feared again. Many people, especially during the Middle Ages, did not understand why we had these magical abilities. And people fear what they don't understand!

In those times, people saw animals through a service-oriented lens. Many couldn't understand our abilities to comprehend the human world through the eyes of a smaller creature. They were used to animals just being there to accomplish certain tasks. The horses would carry you around and get you places. The dogs would be your herders and protectors of your home, and also your loyal companions. Through training, they could perform services for you. We don't discredit that in any form. Dogs are here for a reason and with a wonderful mindset of helping humans in the most apparent ways. The same goes for horses and other animals who even wilfully give their lives as livestock and feeding matter for humans and other animals. We have the highest respect and pay our highest regard to these animals that help you out in these very evident ways. But that is not the way of the cats on this planet.

Cats are here as spiritual companions

We are here as more of a spiritual companion for you humans. Of course, we are also here to represent our species – don't get us wrong. We were seeded here from the heavens to be representatives of your more evolved brothers and sisters that occupy other star systems. But that is a different chapter and for later in the book.

Let's get back to our very earthly existence and task here: to bring the fine energies to this world and to be your friends and companions in every sense of the word. So in the spirit of befriending you in the early times of human civilization, we've grown closer and closer over the decades. We became your loyal friends, but also your healers, your advisers, and your companions during all your endeavors. Yes, we've traveled the seas with your early seafarers. We took care of the mice on board of these ships, but we also provided comfort and purring and a warm loving presence on the ships during the hardships of the journey. We helped colonize the new worlds that you arrived in. We paired with some of the wilder cat species on each continent where we arrived. And this is how the triumph of the cats around the world began!

We were here when you invented the settlements, the farming, the scientific explorations, the land mass explorations, the sea conquering, and all the medical advancements humans achieved in the last 10,000 years – as well as all the schooling, learning, and awakening that you underwent over the decades. We comforted you during the bad times. We were here for you during the Industrial Revolution, during the Renaissance, during the world wars even, and during all the awakening of mankind that took place in the 60s, and ever since. We were here when the triumph of the connected lifestyle began: the internet and social media. Yes, we even became the first social media stars as a species! What would the internet be without cat videos?

And so, to round out this chapter of cats and humans growing together and forming this beautiful relationship of symbiotic coexistence, we were here to accompany you through the good times and the bad times of human evolution. And we are here now to guide you further, into the next phase of your existence: the Great Awakening and the journey onto the next level of consciousness. With this, we are concluding the chapter about the old ways of being and want to guide you into the new ways of being.

THE CAT SECRET

3

YOUR PURPOSE IS TO BE YOU

In our many interactions we've had with humans over the course of time, it has shown itself that when cats are around, humans do their greatest work! So this chapter is all about how we, the cats, get into relationships with humans, and how we are here to inspire them to do their best, or to inspire expression of what is naturally within them. You might call it inspiration, but we are just here to help you express the deepest feelings and depths of yourself. We sit with you when you are in prayer or meditation. We sit with you when you do your work: be it gardening, or cooking, or writing, or painting, or composing music, or just being there for other people, such as caring for your family members. We are there to share your sorrow and hopes and dreams and biggest aspirations. And by being with you or next to you, we infuse you with our spirit, our essence, and our deepest love and empathy. We inspire you to do great things because you see us just being ourselves.

That is one of the biggest learnings or pieces of wisdom we share with humans, and part of what we want to explain in this book: to just be! To be yourself, be who you are, be the one that came into this life to create and be a human being. In short, just *be yourself.*

Cats teach you to just be yourself

We cats often get misinterpreted as being lazy or self-centered or just doing whatever we please. Many people almost fear us because they cannot understand or decipher us; because we seem to have a human-kind free will and because we cannot be boxed in, tamed, or used for your lower human purposes. But this is where the interesting part begins.

To the same extent as many people fear us and almost loathe us – for simply being ourselves – there are even more people who love and revere us for it! We are showing you how to truly just be, and to be who you are here to be. Being a human is to be full of joy and love and creation. Humans come here with the uncanny and quite wonderful ability to create their own circumstances and to create a life full of joy, harmony, and wonders. It's just that you forget all of this when you reincarnate and dive through the veil of human emotion and darkness that is present on this planet. At least that is how it used to be.

We are speaking from a higher form of cat wisdom and knowledge now. We and all of the souls and spirit forms know that everything comes to be because of our will of creation. Everything comes into being as a feeling first: the spark of creation. That's where the will and the free spirit come from. We then willingly and consciously put ourselves into a form, an avatar of flesh or denser matter, so to speak, that can best carry out our intended purpose. We know this beforehand, and we willingly enter an incarnation so we can comprehend life on a denser level, the level of physical creation on planet Earth. It sounds like fun and excitement at first, but we pass through many layers of veil, clouding our judgment and, along the way, we lose some of that free spirit that we naturally are. As we find ourselves in a physical body – human or cat or other – we realize that we are not as free as we should be, and we start to rebel against it. We start to perceive our physical state of being more of a fight or survival or dealing with instincts that tell us to feed and do other lower-level things. That instills in us a feeling of unease or not knowing how to handle this level of existence.

But let us tell you: it all makes sense once you move out of this body into the higher realms of existence! You realize it was a joy to be living in a body. You made experiences you otherwise would have missed out on. The experience of touching, of feeling physically, of living and breathing and loving in a physical body. It's really all a magical adventure! And yes, your soul has learned a thing or two, but it's all a matter of learning to embrace your physical beingness and to make it into the greatest adventure ever. Open your eyes and look at the creation around you. Isn't it wonderful, how you can see colors and breathe the air, how you can see physical objects around you, and even touch them?

The physical experience is like nothing else in the universe. And the layers of forgetting or dampening your instinctual senses are there for a reason, which we won't go into in this book. Suffice it to say that there is so much love and magic on this planet, and there is so much more to come.

Cats are fully aware of their purpose

We, the cats, are part of this experience. We also come into this world not knowing what's going to happen. But we instinctively know that we are here to do something important. We know that we are all part of the grand divine plan which reveals a greater purpose: to help create this world in all its facets and its glory.

For cats, it is fairly easy to understand their purpose in each lifetime. They are inherently born with a wide-open connection to their higher guidance and to that sea of consciousness and creation that we are all part of. Cats are very aware of who they are and what they are here to do, as well as who they are here to support and why.

Humans, on the other hand, are more complex in nature. Due to the intricateness of human society and an upbringing full of man-made rules and childhood imprints, humans tend to lose that inherent connection to their purpose and their abilities of creation. They spend many years or decades, some even a lifetime, to try and understand their purpose.

But this is something they can learn from the cats: to be themselves! Cats are living their highest purpose just by being themselves. And every day of their lives, they are showing humans how you can be you.

And this is not necessarily in the sense of *doing* something but more in the sense of *being YOU*. By being yourself, your purpose will naturally flow through you. And ultimately, we are all here to play together like instruments in an orchestra. Some play the trumpet, some the piano, some the drums. However, one cannot be without the other, or not play the entire symphony. They are all necessary components of a bigger masterpiece. In the same sense, each and every one of us is needed to complete the symphony of this great existence here on Earth and in this part of the galaxy.

Your purpose is about being, not doing

The human concept of *PURPOSE* seems somewhat flawed from our cat's perspective – or, better put, limited. When humans talk about purpose, they are always thinking about *doing* something, like a job or a task or something really important from a human's perspective. It usually springs from the mind. And the more you try to *think* about your purpose and try to figure it out, the more you struggle with the concept.

Your heart, on the other hand, knows. It knows that you are here for a very important reason which you are not necessarily meant to consciously remember. Because it's not about doing and it's not about creating something physical in your world. For some of you, it might be. For others – and we mean the grand majority – it's about *being*. It's about how you put yourself out in the world. It's about how you feel, think, act, and what kind of energy you carry around you. It's about you being in *YOU* mode and not pretending to be someone or something that you are not. It's not about becoming a great executive leader or getting a certain job title. It really isn't.

We cats are around many people who are trying to become someone important in their workplace. And while we are not condemning it – how could we, as we know how great and precious each and every one of our humans is – we usually try to warn them that what they are striving for is not always aligned with their values or the truth of who they are.

Oh, how we see our precious humans laboring away at their computers. How we see them agonize or stress out over their phones and laptops, holding up a facade of who they like to portray themselves as on social media. Putting up a facade in the workplace, trying to solve unsolvable things in their projects, just to prove that they are worthy.

From our cat perspective, it seems so easy! Just relax, put your phone away, go outside, sit in nature, and *ENJOY*! Enjoy the moment, be in the moment, and just let go and let god.

Make no mistake: we cats do understand that your human life is more complicated than our life. That you have all these rules and limitations, and all these statutes and laws you live by. Your life is governed by the clock – the man-made clock – and not by the cycles of nature. We cats do adapt to your rules and lifestyles: we learn to sleep when you sleep and be up when you are. We learn to eat at the clock times that you set for us. And we lovingly do so and abide by many of your rules. And yes, we are happy doing it! Because we live in your world and go with what you set as your schedule.

But – and here comes the *but* – we do wish to tell you that we are lovingly watching over your activities and that we are trying to let you know when we feel that you are exerting yourself. When you are "willing" things into existence without having your heart in it, and when we feel that you are very much out of sync with your true self, with what your body can handle, and with what your soul really yearns for.

That is when the so-called "behavioral problems" of your cats start, and we don't want to go into too much detail at this point. But we cats will let you know when you are not on your highest path, and when we feel your soul self is screaming at you to take a different turn, or to stop doing something, or to start being yourself. Then we cats will "act up" or act weird thereby trying to tell you that there is something wrong – not in our life, but in yours! We are showing you that you are not aligned with your values and your soul path. We'll explain in more detail later in the book when it comes to our feline tasks and purposes with you. At this point, suffice it to say that we cats are very much in tune with our human companions, and we are there to let you know when your human self is not aligned with your soul self.

4

HOW CATS AND HUMANS ARE RELATED

As for our own experience with humans, we can safely say that it is our honor and pleasure to share our lives with you. We cats truly are loving and kind beings at heart. We know that you also see our predator side, pouncing and hunting other creatures, but this was given to us by nature and it's what our physiology makes us out to be. But our souls are pure, as are most humans' souls.

Many of us cats are lovingly sharing our lives and hearts with you. And we are oh so proud of what you have achieved over the past centuries and decades. You've come a long way from being surviving, instinctual beings, much like our feline forefathers and many of us who still live in the wild. But look at what you have created for yourselves! You are now just one step away – in evolutionary terms – to becoming truly enlightened beings.

You are here to learn how to create on a physical level, which is the true masterpiece of creation. Yes, it's easier to create in the higher realms, because just your vibration and your thoughts and wishes will create things and circumstances. But to do so on a physical level and on this plane is a true masterpiece of creation. That is why we can say without a doubt that you, dear humans, are becoming masters. It's what you are truly here for: to create and to push life and creation further on the finest of levels, the physical level. You might say this is the densest of levels, but it only confirms that it's the hardest or the most delicate to do.

What does this have to do with the cats, you might ask? We are just steering your thoughts and emotions into this direction. Let us elaborate.

Cats know about the grand divine plan

The human experience is like nothing else in the Universe. It's bridging your thoughts and emotions as beings on a denser planet into a higher form of existence. You come here knowing nothing of your past, and yet you get to explore life at its finest, without a preconceived notion of anything. You get to start fresh every time you come here and choose a new incarnation! While this exists in a similar fashion on other planets, it's truly a unique experience here for many of you. This is exactly why you chose to come here.

As for us cats, we experience a similar life here. We come into a new kitten body with not much knowledge of what was before. We come knowing of our importance, though, and that we are here to bring love and joy to the joint experience. With which we mean the planetary body, the humankind, the animal kingdoms, the plant kingdoms, the crystalline and mineral realms, and all of the life that teems here on this wonderful planet. We are all in this awakening process together, and we are helping to bring in a new era of peace and enlightenment, a new era of love and enjoying the fruits of our common labor. We've made it through much of the darker ages in this experience, and we are all coming out on top as more loving, caring, and benevolent individuals.

We are jointly going into the new age together. Yes, humans and cats and dogs and horses and all other species. We've made it together this far, and we are well on our way to living in the New Earth.

The cats are here to help move forward the agenda of bringing love, peace, and enlightenment into this part of the galaxy. It's what some of us call the grand divine plan, or what some of you call the Ascension. It's a normal part of existence, with many of these experiences being shared with other planets. There are beings helping and assisting Earth with this process, and we are here in spirit form and in physical form to help you ascend into your own masterpiece of creation: the soul evolving in a body, in a physical avatar, and rising to the next level of experience.

It's something that all humans and animals on Earth are going through right now, and many of us (or you) will go to this next level in your physical incarnation. The part of us cats in it is simple and straightforward: to accompany our humans onto this next level.

Cats have been seeded here from Lyra

Let's go into the *WHY* for a moment, and let us explain how exactly cats and humans are related. Here is a little-known truth about cats which we want to share with you today: the feline form is very much a blueprint for other life forms out there on other planets. We have been seeded here on Earth by our Lyran feline star families.

These feline-looking humanoid beings – or cat people – have been around for eons in the Lyra star system, and they have been doing much exploring of this galaxy and beyond, spreading the feline form throughout the galaxy. They were the early "seafarers", to compare it to your modern civilization. They were the ones who brought life and enlightenment and settlements to many other planetary systems, such as the Sirius system and the Pleiades. The feline humanoid races helped other planets and civilizations with building societies of peace, hope, and technology, to advance physically, emotionally, and spiritually. The felines are also the forefathers of humans in many ways, though not alone.

The human race also has a lot of DNA from other star nations that they have been infused with. There are the Arcturians and the Pleidians, which in many ways are also feline infused. There are, of course, the Sirians, which are a conglomerate themselves, of felines, of aquatics, and other species. There are the Orions and other neighbors. And then there are many others that gave their DNA into the human experience. This mix of different genetic markers makes the humans a lifeform with heightened senses and heightened abilities. It also makes them quite diverse in their polarity. Let's elaborate.

The "darker" aspects of the DNA mix in the human gene pool come from the reptilians and other star families in that spectrum. They are part of this universal experience, just like the more loving life forms. At some point, they splintered from Source in a way that was not foreseen in its extremity. They were then sequestered into a different quadrant, to be among themselves where they could be who they were or chose to be. They eventually chose to come into your quadrant, in order to conquer more territory. It's in their genes to do so.

This sparked wars and conflicts with the lighter and higher life forms, in what you might know as the Lyran and Orion wars. The felines had to give way to many of their planetary systems and territories. Some of you in human form do remember these times, and yes, the felines have very much prevailed. They went to other star systems and rebuilt their societies, some even better and stronger and more protected than before. They bonded with the Sirians and built great societies

27

there, while also collaborating with the Pleidians and other star systems.

With the variety of different life forms in this galaxy and its ongoing conflicts, Earth was chosen as a middle ground and made into what you call a peace treaty. Humans were chosen to combine all of our strengths to become one super life form: the strength, resilience, and resolve of the reptilians and their like, and the kindness and love capabilities of the more benevolent life forms, such as the felines and their like.

Earth was then sequestered to go through this experience without any interference from the outside. Your human DNA was infused over time, from the early human-like beings on Earth, into the human race as you know it today. The project has been monitored by the different star nations, with some more interfering than others. The reptilians pushed it further into something of "policing" the experience, and the more benevolent nations gave them more leeway than originally planned. But let's continue this galactic history at some later point in the book, and return to the feline part in the humans' development.

The Lyrans, the cat people, have been at the forefront of this experience from the get-go. We gave much of our genome into the human field and bodies. The cats on Earth, as you know them in their four-legged form, were left here as your animal companions and as a reminder of who you truly are, and that there is a large part of feline genes in you. Our DNA is what gives you your capability of love and joy, amongst other things. We are the ones that infused you with ancient knowledge of other civilizations on other planets. We are also the healers and the energy workers and the knowers of other lifetimes and life forms. Our DNA is very much alive in you, and more and more humans are waking up to their feline ancestry. It starts out small, by loving us, the cats, in special ways. Then, by spending time with us, a knowing of *MORE* becomes more prevalent in you. Then, eventually, you understand that we are very much alike. That cats and humans are closely related, in a genome kind of way, but also in their antics, personalities, and in their way of seeking wisdom and enlightenment.

Your cat helps you to be in the moment

Look at your own cats: how often do they show you that you need to relax and let go? To sit down quietly and just enjoy your day? To let go of all the stress and just sit and "roll around" and clean yourself and just let go and let god? These traits of cats are there to remind you to find your stillness. Your beingness. Your being in the moment. And not let your stress and worries get the best of you, not let your outside world dictate your day or your life. To stay centered, to stay *YOU*, and to remain calm or find your calm even in the most unfortunate circumstances. Your cat will show you to be in the moment, no matter what.

We cats are true masters of enjoying the moment, and this is what we want to tell our humans: be in the here and now! Don't worry about yesterday, or the should have's, could have's, would have's. Don't worry about tomorrow. We live today. This is something the cats can teach you. Just be who you are today.

It's really all about being in the moment. Humans are always thinking about the past and future, and what they have to do. We cats are here to help you find an equilibrium, a point you can return to, like a point of reference, if you may. When our humans get stressed out or overthink, then we get on their laps or meow to them... telling them: touch me, bring your attention to me. It brings you back into the moment, away from your thoughts and challenges of life. We help you focus on us, so you can come back into the here and now.

And while we love the interaction with our humans – we are hedonists by nature – we are aware that we both benefit from these encounters. We cats get the attention and the cuddles, and you humans come back into the moment. You feel our soft fur. You hear our purring. Your eyes relish at the beauty of us. Your heart goes out to how cute we are. All your senses are engaged as you stroke us or sit down with us. There is no room for heavy thoughts or worry, as you hold us and feel us in your arms. And as we are both enjoying the interaction, you can now see how we cats help you be in the moment and just be who you are right now.

5

THE THREE MAIN TASKS OF CATS

In this chapter, we wish to elaborate more on our tasks with our beloved humans. Apart from upholding the feline essence and being your close companion to remind you of your galactic lineage, we cats are here for other important reasons. While we'll explain our individual tasks later in the book, we want to talk about the three main tasks of cats in the Ascension process.

Upholding the frequency of love and joy

The first one is very simple, which makes it so grand. We cats are here to bring love and joy into this realm – for humans, mostly, but also for other animals and for the planet. We enrich the shared field with love and joy. Love meaning, our love and our lust for life itself. We just *love* to *be*! We love life. We love to get up and explore. We love to touch things with our paws, with our tactile system, with our whiskers. We love to use all our senses. The sniffing and detecting of even the faintest scents in the air around us. The tilting of the head and the head bumping. Rubbing ourselves against objects, against the ground. Scratching and stretching, putting our claws into trees and smelling, feeling the tree, and feeling its unique vibration and beingness. Everything in nature has a distinct scent, a distinct feel, a distinct look (which is more important for humans than us felines), but the point is that everything in nature has a distinct vibration, or let's call it a vibe. This vibe is what makes this planet and this world here so vibrant, if we may use a human term.

We are here to explore and to love what we do, what we see, and what we experience. We cats are true masters in that! We explore the world with all our senses. We lay still in the grass and might not "do" anything, but make no mistake: all of our senses are highly active! We feel the grass under our bellies, we hear the sounds of the birds in the distance, we smell the faintest of flowers or herbs in the area, and we revel in the beauty of all of it, of nature, of creation, and the sheer being of existence! We feel the feeling in our bellies when we are hungry. We recognize the wonder and the beauty in an insect flying by. Just the sheer miracle that it is all alive and vibrant! It brings us joy to just lay there and take it all in – the miracle of being, the miracle of being alive.

Yes, we cats love to be alive! We love to use all of our senses. We love to just be and to influence others with our happiness and joy of being. So this is where our humans come in, and our important – oh so important – task with our humans. Our main job with humans is to just be with you. That's it. As easy as that! Everything else comes second. The main task is *very* important to us. It is so crucial that we spend part of our lives closely being with you, sitting with you, lying with you, letting you pet us, and playing with you. Just being around you, our humans, gives us immense pleasure and joy.

Attuning you to our frequency

This brings us to our second task in the global Ascension process if you can separate the two tasks. For us, it's pretty much the same thing, but for your human mind, we know how you like to dissect and understand things in their finer nature. The second task is to influence you or to attune you to our frequencies. Just by being around you, you usually attune to our frequencies! We act like a tuning fork, and you'll pick up on our "good" vibes and you'll automatically elevate your frequency.

It's one of the beautiful things in nature or in this vibrational Universe, that the one with the lower frequency will always strive to match the one with the higher frequency. It's one of the laws of nature. And your whole beingness and your wonderful soul plan knows that you want to be in a higher and more elevated state, which is your normal state as a soul anyway. So in your human form, when being bogged down by daily life and all the things that seem to make your existence here harder than it needs to be, when all these things bring down your joyful state of being and your overall vibration in this human body and mind, then we cats come in as your tuning fork! We'll sit with you and spend time around you, thus "forcing" your vibration to naturally elevate. That's part of the magic of cats, and why cat people just *love* to be around cats. We naturally make you feel better, but to this day you couldn't explain why. So now you know: we act as your tuning fork, and you'll naturally raise your vibration the longer you spend time with us.

So there you have it. These are the two most important things that we cats "do" for humans on this earthly plane. We enrich their field with love (of being alive) and with joy (for a more joyful way of being). You achieve this just by being around us and vibrationally attuning to us. But you also do this by watching us: our zest for life, our love of exploring, our joy of using all our senses, and our sometimes childlike nature of being in awe, wonder, and a joyful way of experiencing life.

Accompanying you through life

Let's assure you at this point that we cats know what we do on the larger scale of things, but we also want to say that we really *love* our humans, no doubt about that. And this love prevails over everything, even over the fact that many cats pass earlier than their beloved humans. We'd like to say this is an evolutionary thing, and there is no particular reason why, biologically, cats won't get older and older in years to come, with proper medical care and the enhanced healing powers of this planet. There will be a time when cats will grow much older than the usual 15-20 year lifespan they have now.

But until then, it's important for our beloved humans to know that our love and our service to you do not end when our physical bodies expire. Our love prevails and is still there for you on the other side! Our souls are not bound by this physical body or incarnation. We are transcending space and time in our soul or spirit form. When we pass away, meaning when our physical vessel expires, our souls come out of this form completely unscathed. We cross the dimensions and realms and go back into our spirit form, which is much freer and easier to be in than the physical vessel. But it still means that we are bound to this earth or planet until our souls are free of the contracts and agreements we've made while incarnated by your side.

So, chances are that we'll stay around for many years to come. We either watch over you from the other side, or we work with and sometimes *through* the new cats that are physically by your side. We sometimes even come into your new cats in our spirit form. In a sense, we slip into the other cat's body for a while, just so that we can sit or sleep on your bed again. (The other cats don't mind, we can peacefully coexist for a few minutes, or sometimes even hours or days). It makes *YOU* feel at ease, and it once again uplevels your vibration, when we can physically be with you again for a short time. Each one of you has probably experienced it: you are thinking of your beloved cat friend that crossed over, but you could swear to see him in your new cat as he sleeps beside you. Or your new cat meows or rubs herself against you in a way that only we used to do. And no, you are not imagining it. In those moments, we are truly with you. Our soul essence is coming through to you in your new cat, and in these moments we are as close as we used to be. We do this for you, but we also enjoy those moments of physical closeness again.

In any case, chances are that – after we cross over – we stick around with you for quite a while. We watch over you. We hold or enrich the energies around you. Yes, we are capable of doing this from the other side, and sometimes even better than before, because we are not bound by a physical vessel, but we are much bigger on the other side. We also work closely with your "now" cats and help them guard you, assist you, and accompany you. We pass on some of our tasks to your current cats, and we work through them, with them and together, so you can be all that you can be, and live your life to the fullest and to the happiest. Because it's all about happiness and joy for us!

Sometimes, or let's say many times, we also come back to you in a new body. And while we are not exactly the same cat or the same personality as before, we usually come close enough. We come back to our humans in a new form, as our old cat form expired and couldn't match your lifespan. But we found a way of accompanying you through your life anyway and continuing our task with you through simply reincarnating and then finding our way back to you.

You have suspected it before. That your *now* cat acts just like the cat from your childhood. Or maybe it wasn't even the action... it might just be the *feeling* that you have in their presence. That feeling of knowing, of deep belonging, of being comfortable in each other's presence like in no one else's. Just know that we cats come back to you in many forms: as other cats (same or similar looks), or in a dog body (when you cannot have a cat in that phase of your life), or even in a horse body. We can even manage to cross with other mammals, but won't go into that now. Yes, cats are cats are cats, but there are some "physical body" thresholds that can be crossed in the form of love.

So we come back to you in new incarnations, until our tasks or missions or soul contracts are fulfilled, and when both our souls are in agreement and at ease with us parting ways. That is when we dissolve our existing contracts, and we both move on. Until that moment, we love each other so much that we'll just stay together until we are both fulfilled. Afterwards, our love for each other parts ways, so we can both make the world brighter by shining our light on others and taking on tasks with someone else who requires our assistance or can benefit from our presence in their lives – in physical or spirit form.

This concludes the chapter on cats and their humans and our three main tasks with humans: 1. Spreading love and joy in the world, 2. Elevating your vibration to match ours, and 3. Accompanying you throughout your life, until we both agree to having fulfilled our highest commitment for each other – or in other words, having reached such a level of love beyond measure and unconditional love that we can move on to higher levels.

6

ABOUT PURPOSEFUL CREATION

Before we go into the more detailed and individual purr-poses of cats, let's recap: the cats' bigger mission is to be in the love and joy frequencies, not only for themselves and their kind, but also for the planet, for the humans, and for the whole planetary evolution as well.

The other animals have their own way of putting their energy out there. We are not touching on other animals' tasks, as we are only speaking for ourselves in this book. But suffice it to say, that each one of them has their plan and their own frequency to uphold. As for the cats, we can share that this is our plan for mankind and for the grand divine plan, or the Ascension process, as you call it.

In conclusion, cat beings came here to Earth many millennia ago, and their task has been passed on to some of their predecessors, or the cats as you know them now, in order to share their ancient wisdom from other planets and cultures, and to be there when humankind awakens to their true selves and to their powers of creating their world with love and joy.

Humans are here to create on a physical level

Humans are also here as part of the grand divine plan, and their part is creation and expansion, not only of their physical livelihood but mostly of their non-physical soul expression. This includes (but is not limited to) their special way of creating things out of seemingly nowhere, where their minds conceive something (an idea, a thought, a concept), and their hands in conjunction with their minds and hearts (very important, this is the source and an important part of creation), will literally make something out of nothing. It first comes as an idea, a spark of inspiration. Then your heart knows it is the right thing to do, and you really want to bring this great idea, this creation of yours, into the world. And then your hands – and your feet – get going and your whole body and your whole beingness is involved in bringing this thing into creation that your mind wants to see done and your heart truly wants to see, feel, and touch in front of you.

This goes for all of mankind's creations, starting from homes, to cars, to other means of transportation, to all your means of communication, to schools to law institutions, etc. And then spanning to all the non-material things, such as your social networks, your TVs, your clubs and associations, and all the immaterial but oh-so-important things that contribute to your civilization. All of your creations come and work together in conjunction, and just like that, a new civilization is born on this beautiful planet, which is not only the backdrop but also your mother and an essential part of your creation. This "new" planet then goes out and becomes a part of the universal civilization, meeting other civilizations out there and becoming a member of the universal society of life, where different nations or life forms are gathering together to make this creation even bigger and vaster, and teeming with life and creation and ideas and, of course, togetherness. This might be part of a more advanced book, but we wanted to give you a glimpse of what is being shared with you.

Cats are here to create on a vibratory level

Going back to the cats and the *NOW* times... let's briefly touch on the cats' contribution or way of creation. It is a bit different from yours. We cats are not as knowledgeable in this cat form that we came here in. Meaning, we do not build planes or cars or do all these things with our hands or paws. But we do have vibrational capabilities of creation. We help humans *create* in their own special ways, by being their partners, their inspirations, their wayshowers. By sitting with you when you do your creating, be it from the mind or from the heart. By being your loving supporters, by helping you with your healings, by healing your heart, by transmuting the energies around you, by inspiring you to be you and to be free. We are here for you in all the ways that we'll be describing in the chapters to come, about our individual cat purr-poses. For now, suffice it to say that humans in their form have special ways of creating physical things. While we cats in our form here have our own way of creating our environment: from the heart and just by being in a certain vibratory state.

In the next chapters, we are going to talk about how cats and humans are in on this together, and how we cats support humans in our own special ways. This is the individual cat's purr-pose part. We are going to share our own special contributions, as each one of us is a soul with a distinct purr-pose with our humans.

First, we want you to know that we really appreciate your love and reverence for us. We love it that you care for us so much. We love it that you are in wonder of us. We love it that you give us names and have us live in your homes, in joint unison and, in many cases, as an actual family member. We love our humans! Make no mistake, different from common lore or what many people think: yes, we do love our humans very much! We might have a different way of showing it from, say, a dog. They are more in tune with your wishes and your commands, and they'll please you and expect you to command them. They are your loyal companions, much in a way a horse would be if horses were still around you like they used to. Horses and dogs have an important task with you: they serve you, protect you, and help you along in your daily life.

We cats differ a bit in our tasks with you, but nevertheless, we do have a task: we help our humans along their journey of becoming an adult, becoming a member of society, finding a job, finding their footing in life, and – most importantly – pursuing what they love!

Cats live fully in their purr-pose

Yes, we have finally arrived at the topic of purpose. We cats very much understand this concept, as it is true and close to our hearts. We, of course, are not just here to eat and sleep and play and be cute. We have a much bigger task, and we are here to help our humans make this world go round – literally!

We are here to help our humans be happy and happily go about their lives, and find joy in everything that they do. To be content and to be grateful, but also to push along, to explore boundaries and beyond, and to just simply be in beautiful, graceful, and purposeful creation.

Let's talk more about the concept of purpose. We have already elaborated on the concept of creation, so this is our next step in explaining our close companionship with humans.

In our world, the word purpose means nothing more but being in purposeful creation of who you are. When you are creating, there is always a purpose behind it. There is always something that you intend to do or be or something that you want to achieve. When you are doing something with purpose, you are generally in line or in tune with your nature, otherwise you wouldn't want to do it. If you are not creating in joy and aligning with your nature – or purpose – of why you're here, then what would be the point in doing it?

It's the utmost thing to be or do when you create with purpose. When you are in tune with who you are and what your soul essence brings forth, then you are an unstoppable force of nature. You are in your purpose. You act with purpose. You go forth with purpose. You live your purpose. You live purposefully. You live *with* purpose!

That's all anyone ever strives to do: live with purpose. Live aligned with your values, with your true nature, with your beingness. So our concept of purpose is a little bit different from how humans interpret it. Yes, we understand purpose as something you are born with, and then you proceed to act on it. The acting comes *after* the being your own purposeful creation. The action comes from your purposeful way of putting yourself out there, and how you understand yourself in the world.

So do cats come with purpose? Of course! Otherwise, what would be the point in existing and coming into this world, where everything is interwoven and magically connected? The cats come into this lifetime just as purposeful as the humans, and we'll explain in a minute how this is all connected.

7

CATS AND THEIR PURR-POSE

Not too long ago, we cats were in a state of just being and just being ourselves. That was before this wave of awakening hit planet Earth. So let's say our story of awakening, together with humans, and our growing awareness of what we are here to do and who we are as souls – individual soul and soul group – came more to the forefront of our being. We became more aware that there was a bigger picture out there for us, and a specific thing that we were supposed to contribute, similar to humans, who started to find their way back to Source, wholeness, or the Ascension process.

In the 60s and 70s, we experienced an early awakening of mankind, with a growing understanding that there was something out there for play, fun, individualism, and a huge sense of personal freedom. Meaning freedom from conventions, from rules, from society standards, from everything keeping them in a box. Then, in the 80s, came a time of professionalism and also personal space to grow as a person. In the 90s, the personal freedom of expression grew even bigger.

So let's say the cats' path to awakening followed – or you could also say complemented – the human state of consciousness, of becoming bigger, better, more compassionate, more conscious, of the environment, the planet, the fellow people, the animals, and of being part of something special that was worth preserving and enhancing and protecting, but also evolving. With the dawn of the internet in the 90s, personal freedom of expression and being who you are received a new burst, as the growing internet and the limitless expression and connection through social media spawned the dawn of the true awakening of mankind.

By the same token, or in the same flow of things, the cats became more aware of who they are and how they are here to help and push and nudge their humans into all that they are, and all that they are here to do!

When the true Ascension energies hit the planet, many say around 2012, with the unique cosmic alignments, it was the start of something beautiful, something new, something never been done before. An Ascension of a planetary body, with all its beings in their physical avatars, intact and ready to move into the next level of beingness, of consciousness, of vibration – all while being in a physical body.

It has been done before on other planetary systems. Sirius has gone through a similar process, but not with so many species on the planet, and with such little influence from outside, and without disturbing the surface of the planet – the trees, the water, the land masses, etc.

Yes, your Ascension is happening organically, with as little damage as possible to the land masses and the bodies of water, and all the species living here. It is done in surgical parts, so that the living beingness and all the goodness that has been built here outside of and within humanity and the animal species won't be disrupted, but gently moved forward. So everything you see happening, the Earth changes *are* indeed happening, yet from a higher perspective we know that there is a reason and purpose behind it. And all the ones losing their physical lives are being brought to the other side where they can ascend higher. It is not a punishment for them and for the land, but a moving forward of this global plan of Ascension and evolution for humans, animals, plants, and minerals alike.

The cats' side of the awakening process

So we cats have been awakening together with the humans in the last 20 years. We became more conscious of who we are and what we are here to do. We as a species evolved spiritually, emotionally, and also mentally. We became more intelligent, as human scientists would put it. We don't only understand your words and meanings. Since we are living so closely with humans, we understand your entire world better than you think.

We cats do understand you have "work" to do. We understand you follow a set of rules and regulations that you – or society – have set up for you. We understand you have a "job" to do and that you have to leave the house to do things that are beyond our conscious comprehension. So yes, we know and understand there are things beyond our horizon of cats, but it doesn't really matter. What we *do* understand is that humans are wonderful, heartfelt beings who are here with the best of intentions. That most of them love us, and that they allow us or bring us into their homes, so we can be part of their family life. Part of the upbringing of their children and part of passing on values and love and joy to others.

This is where we become an essential part of your lives. We become part of your creations or your purpose in life. We understand how you are bigger than just your body, and bigger than all the rules that humanity puts on you. We know you inside out. We know and recognize your fears. Your fears of putting yourself out there as an individual with your thoughts, opinions, feelings, ideas, and emotions. We know you are here to do something very important: to be part of evolution, to bring in your special gifts and talents, and to be *YOU* to the core.

Since we cats are masters in being ourselves, this is something that we truly understand you need to do: be you! Don't let anyone put a label on you, don't put too many labels on yourself! Your creations are your creations are your creations. No one else creates them like you. And don't put yourself in a box trying to fit your creations into what pleases other people. Each one of you is unique, and you don't need to make it smaller than it is, what you do in life, and what you create.

That being said, let's now move on to our purpose as cats. We *are* here to be ourselves. We *are* here to contribute something special. We *are* here, each one of us, with a beautiful, unique, and heartfelt purr-pose.

These cat purr-poses can be quite individual in each case. While our bigger mission is to inspire *YOU* to be yourself (as explained in the previous chapters), our individual purpose has to do with our individual journeys, but of course also *your* journeys! Our humans are usually part of our purpose, at least for those cats that live closely with humans. So let's elaborate on that, and for the next few chapters, we are going to focus on those of us that live in close conjunction with humans, as part of their family and part of their path. We'll also explain how closely they are entwined with their humans on a heart and soul level.

So let's begin. Part of being a cat in this day and age is the beautiful and wonderful task of sharing their life with a human. This human is usually our pride and joy, much like you humans take pride in us or in your children. Yes, we said it: you, the human, are the pride and joy in our life! While our life usually revolves around you, it is fair to say that we are here with a specific purpose to keep our humans happy, emotionally safe, and filled with joy and love in their hearts. We do this in our own special ways.

The soul essence groups of cats

While each one of us cats is quite unique, there is an underlying commonality in what we do for our humans. We have been categorized in breeds, coat colors, or other outward categories before, but that does not really do it justice. It is merely a compilation of outward appearance traits and somewhat superficial characteristics that humans have put on us.

A disclaimer: we do not disrespect the cat breed categorizations, and matter of fact, we are quite flattered that you are putting so much emphasis on exploring our personalities and traits and beautiful color and coat schemes. Yet the *real* differences don't lie in our outward appearance – they lie inwards and in our unique blueprints of life. The real difference is in our beingness as a soul, with our soul purr-pose and soul contracts.

So let's elaborate on what we are here to do, and how we fulfill our destiny or purpose with our humans.

8

THE 12 CAT ARCHETYPES

T he following distinction of our soul essence types is quite magical and powerful, and it gives people a good idea of who we are. Some of these archetypes are unique to us cats. Some of the categories also fit dogs or horses, or even humans, if you wish to explore further. Yet this book is about us cats, and for you as a cat lover, here is our very own categorization of what we are here to do for you humans.

Let's start with the obvious one:

❧ THE LOVER

This archetype is one of the most common ones, and it overlaps with many of the others. Suffice it to say that in one way or another, all of us cats – like all humans – are here to love each other. To find love, to teach love, to feel love, and to *be* love. As everything in this Universe consists of love, it is quite obvious that love is the essence of our being. Ours, yours, and everyone's in this grand divine plan. Love is the building block of the Universe. Love is all there is!

So it's not surprising that the lover archetype is one of the most common ones, and many other archetypes overlap with it. But let's get into more detail about the genuine lover cat archetype.

They are here to *love*. They are here to give. They are here to hang around you a lot, to comfort you when you are down. But also to be there to celebrate your wins and your good times. They are here to be at your side during the good news and the bad news you receive. During your uptimes and your downtimes. They will always be by your side, and they will always shower you with love and affection.

These cats are quite magical in their complexity and also in their simplicity. The lovers are givers but also bringers of joy. They give unconditional love and also teach it. They are there for you, come hell and high water, and through thick and thin.

The lover is a great cat to have around. He is mostly in a higher frequency, or in his physical expression, in a joyful, relaxed, and loving mood. He is oozing and spreading love, while he is sitting next to you or laying next to you, while sleeping or dozing, or in his wake state. The lover is always there for you, and always sharing moments with you.

When you are coming home distraught or stressed out from work, then he will be there to catch you. He will be lifting your mood instantly, just by you looking into his eyes! It will uplift your spirits, your heart, your soul, and your entire being. By rubbing himself against you, he will help you release stress. By stroking his shiny, soft fur, you will be releasing oxytocin hormones. You will be holding onto his soft body, and feel him next to you. You will not only be hormonally refreshed and at ease, but also mentally and spiritually renewed. The lover is a pure loving essence of himself, as we are all born with and as we are all going back to after our physical body dies. So in a sense, we are all lovers! But some of us come in their purest soul essence and embody their highest and truest selves.

The lover cats are usually in a pure and high vibration. Some might feel as having almost angelic vibes. This is how we help our human get through the ups and downs of his life – by being in a pure state, in an almost angelic frequency, or in our purest frequency of love.

The lover might also be there not just to give or embody love but also to help someone love – even love themselves, for instance. Many people come with a vow of not loving themselves, because of the collective burdens or issues that are still prevalent in the human field from millennia ago. So many of you come with the task of lightening that topic in the human field, and ideally, purging it out of your own field, and by doing so lightening the charge in the collective field. And in its highest form, by overcoming this issue in yourself, you can help others overcome it too! So your task is not only to purge it for yourself but to help others do the same until there is no more of that issue in the field. That goes for all of the "core wound" topics that humans are born with. And many animals come with these "core wounds" as well. This is how we help humans clear their field of the issues that humanity has collected in many millennia of being in their older form, so you can be upgraded to the newer form, or the new human, as we are speaking.

So in the case of a human whose task is to purge and work through the issue of self-love, we cats come in our highest and purest form to help you understand that being in a state of love is your true nature. And as we explained earlier, in the law of nature of tuning, usually the lower vibrating being will adjust to the higher vibrating being. So by being around us lovers, you'll be able to vibe in the frequencies of pure, unconditional love, and we'll attune you – slowly but steadily – to also reach into the higher love frequencies and become more of what you truly are.

The lovers are also here to attune other animals – cats, dogs, other pets, yes, even horses – to the love frequencies. While upholding these frequencies is not a task for cats alone, we cats collectively contribute to elevating the love frequencies on this planet.

So let us conclude and summarize: the lover cats are here to give unconditional love, thereby not only elevating your mood but also your frequency in the long run. We are also part of the group of beings purging the issues of lack of love, lack of self-love, lack of empathy for other beings, etc., out of the human field, and ultimately, the planetary field. This is a task we share with many other beings.

But we can also teach someone how to love! We can awaken someone's heart that has been closed due to suffering, and we can lead someone who has forgotten how to love back to the path of loving. By looking into our deep and loving eyes, we can awaken someone's heart and have people love us, even if they cannot yet love human beings. We are a precursor of that person letting true love back into his field and his existence. This is the power of cats or other animals (*we don't want to take all the credit here*).

Suffice it to say that we cats know how to sneak into someone's heart and how to bring a smile to someone's face just by being ourselves, by being playful, by showing love, by showing trust, and by loving our humans unconditionally.

This brings us to our next archetype:

🐾 THE JOYBRINGER

Oh, how we love this one! Of course, the description of this archetype can go hand in hand with much of what we said about the lover. Because *JOY* is also of the highest frequency, and in the higher realms, love and joy are almost on the same frequency, or much of the same thing.

So you could say that, as much as the lover brings love, the joybringer brings joy into our human's lives. And this is not a small feat! Your human society has created a culture of tasks, and rules, devoid of the nice and pleasant things of life in many ways. We see our humans labor away at their computers and devices. We see them slave over housework and other tasks you do with your hands. We see or feel you go to an office and sit in a cubicle, where chores are taking all the lifeblood out of work and your life.

That is where we come in to bring more joy into your life. In short: joy is the precursor to love, or love is the pinnacle of joy. Both are entwined and therefore of the highest frequency. And not to forget, both are of the highest and utmost importance for humans and for the entire planet!

When you have a joybringer cat in your life, then you are truly blessed, for you have invited the highest vibration into your home and your heart. The joybringer cats are full of life. They lift your spirits, and they entertain you. Some might have funny antics that make you laugh. Some are just so incredibly cute that you cannot stop smiling when you see them. And some might just be breathtakingly beautiful, and your jaw drops in disbelief at how truly wonderful this cat is.

The joybringers walk the earth with a sense of purpose and passion for everything they do. They have a pep in their step like no other cat. *(This is what the joybringers are saying, while the other cats are smirking).* But truly, they are quite magnificent and so much fun to be around! A joybringer will bring a sense of light to the darkest of places and moments. Even if you are not doing well at all – physically or mentally or emotionally – the joybringer will lighten up your moments. When he rubs himself against you, when he gives you his heart and shares with you his unique way of being, then you are truly blessed.

The joybringer will be playful when you are down and out. They will perform a dance or some cute moves when you are grumpy or angry. They will be rolling around or prancing in front of you when you need cheering up. At this point, we want to make a distinction: joybringers can be a bit more distant in a way that a lover wouldn't. The joybringer can either be very cuddly and give you physical joy moments by being all over you with love bites and lots of cuddling. Or he can "perform" for you at more of a distance but still make your heart sing. You cannot *NOT* be enchanted by a joybringer – *ever!*

Let's recap the joybinger's very important task: he will be in your life when you go through a challenging or stressful time period. He will lighten up your life and reduce your stress level by being his cute, funny, or beautiful self. He will be there for you when you are down. He will read your emotions and play the opposite back to you. Yes, this is quite an amazing feat! The joybringer will also always inherently know what kind of "performance" you need, or what kind of feeling he needs to entice in you. This version of the joybringer, in his purest form, is a magical, very empathic being, but at the same time, he needs to be immune to taking on or mirroring your emotions or moods. For if he took them on, then he would not be in his essence of joy, love, and ease. So they are rarely true empaths, but they have the magical ability to stay true to themselves, to rest fully in their power and who they are, and still be a really good friend and life companion for you.

To clarify: it's all about joy anyway! As we explained earlier, the concept of joy is as important as the concept of love. And we cats are *all* on the mission to spread love and joy for humans. So in that sense, all cats are essentially joybringers. But for the purpose of this categorization and distinction of soul essence archetypes, we are talking about the purest of the purest of the purest joybringers. So let's move on.

The joybringers among us also know how to hold the energies around our family. We are here to uphold a certain frequency around our humans (specifically, the frequency of joy), and we work our magic also for other cats or dogs in the family. Even on a bigger scale: we are essentially here to uphold and elevate the frequency of joy on the planet. By being our magical, intense selves, we hold a high frequency which we feed into the grid of the planet, thereby – and by the law of vibration – being a tuning fork for humans to elevate their joy frequency as well. By doing so, we act as divine tuning forks for much of humanity but also for other animals. We can safely say that this is a feat that is innate to us cats! While dogs bring more of the loyal and protective element to humanity, we cats are here for joy. Love is also the domain of dogs, but joy is certainly ours!

It's not by accident that cat videos are the most cherished videos on YouTube. Cats became YouTube stars long before YouTube grew into the huge entertainment and infotainment machine that it is now. Yes, we cats are a little bit proud of our accomplishment *(smiling coyly)*, but let's get back to the topic at hand.

Joy is a divine thing, the birthright of humans and all beings in existence. Love and joy are the two – or the one – true form of existence! *JOY* is the utmost thing to strive for. It's easier to get someone to feel *JOY* (or its lower form, happiness, which seems more accessible to many people in their current form of existence) than it is to feel or achieve a state of *LOVE*. So let's give you this advice: strive for *JOY* before you strive for unconditional *LOVE*. It's easier, more accessible, and more real in many people's lives. Once you achieve to be in a state of joy many days in a row, then you can move on to *LOVE* and unconditional love – for yourself, for others, and for life itself.

🐾 THE SUPPORTER

This cat archetype is a much-cherished member of our cat collective. They have been with humans since the beginning of mankind. They were literally the first to settle with humans, even without knowing that they had a purpose with them. At that time, 10,000 years ago, the cats – just like their human counterparts – were more instinctive in nature. They were following their survival instincts, and much of their lives revolved around eating, sleeping, foraging, and caring for their offsprings. So when they encountered the first human dwellings, they saw that mice and other rodents abound and they moved into these areas. Soon, they realized that the humans – bipeds – were a friendly race and that they recognized what the cats were doing for them. Thus, a subtle bond of partnership began to form between these early settlers and the early version of the now house cats, as you know them. The cats appreciated the feasting in the humans' dwellings, in equal measures as the humans appreciated their corn and grain stashes being saved from rodent infestation by these quite friendly and pleasing-looking cats.

So we – the cats – moved into their hearts and their homes, and the bond of friendship grew stronger and stronger over the years. We realized that humans would feed us and name us and care for us and our offspring. In return, we would keep their sheds clean and purr for them at their hearths, thus bringing in healing and soothing frequencies, which at the time were not known yet. But as the friendship grew stronger, so did the caring for each other. Therefore, the supporter in all his expression was one of the earliest companions of humans.

When cats became more popular in the more modern times, humans would become fully aware of how cats were there for them emotionally, mentally, and also physically. By stroking our soft fur, hearing our endearing purring, and looking into our deep, soulful eyes, humans can calm down, relax, and feel truly seen and loved. Even if the whole world seems to come crumbling down on them, when a cat lover looks into his cat's eyes, they will see the sun and feel the depth of the ocean, and the depth of our hearts.

Of course, the supporter cat is also an equivalent in bringing love and joy to their humans, but their task goes beyond "just" the love. In modern times, the supporters are quite multitasking, as you would say, or busybodies, if you want to be a bit more humorous. The supporter will be there in all walks of life for his human. He will start off the day by greeting you, cuddling with you, and walking around with you, following you even into the bathroom as you get ready for your day. If you work from home, then your supporter cat will most likely sit next to you, walk over your laptop when needed (telling you to take a break), or warm your seat while you get up for the break. If you leave your home for work, then your supporter cat will greet you at the door in the evening and then follow you around, almost like a dog. He will then close the evening by sitting on your lap or next to you, and then – of course – go to bed with you, not letting you out of his sight.

This is how the supporter does his job: by being there for you around the clock. His presence is soothing to you, his love and caring for you is palpable, and his affection clearly showing. However, the supporter is not just there for you physically or during your everyday schedule. He will also sense or know when you are not doing well or when you are emotionally compromised. He will then go into full care mode by rubbing himself against you, by telling you to cuddle with him, by sitting on your lap, by demanding your attention, and by simply sitting with you while you go through your emotional ups and downs.

Of course, the supporter will also support you during all stages and eras of your life. He will be there when you get your first job, he will guide you through your new relationship, he will sit through heartaches and job changes with you, and he will be by your side through all things that come your way. He is in many ways your anchor, your compass, and the rock in your life. When new partners come and go, when jobs change, when your life goes through ups and downs... even when friends or family members seem to let you down... your supporter cat will *always* be by your side, holding you, comforting you, cheering you up, and in short, supporting you.

This is the most caring cat you'll ever have, and the biggest emotional support you can think of, for they are very empathic and very much tuned into your moods, emotions, and personality traits. The supporter cat will know – without a doubt and like a barometer – before you know yourself, how you feel, and when you need someone to support you. He will come to sit with you even before you realize that you are upset. He will magically show up when you go into a stressful frenzy, and demand to sit on your lap or crawl under your shirt. He will "force" you to sit still with him for a while until he can feel your nervous system calm down and you relax. Then, and only then, will he get up and let you carry on, to go do whatever you were planning on doing before he stopped you in your tracks.

We can conclude this wonderful archetype by saying that the supporter is one of the backbones of the cat collective and one of the most important examples of our species. Without the supporter, there would not be the close bond between cats and humans, and we would be worse off or not be the intellectually highly evolved species that we are.

At this point, we'd like to thank all humans who have supported us the way you have: by caring for us and by inviting us into your homes. By letting us be who we want to be! Yes, we really appreciate that humans are not trying to tell us what to do, or better yet, to put us on a leash or teach us tricks. While some of us actually enjoy the tricks and the clicker training, most of us cats have an expressed sense of dignity and independence, and we really do appreciate it that you let us just be. Meaning that we get to spend our days as we wish, and we get to do our jobs as we see fit or as we feel they need to be done.

With this, we'll conclude this important species in our midst, and we'd like to move on to the next representative.

🐾 THE SOULMATE

This archetype seems to be quite similar to the supporter in many ways and you might think they are one of the same. But there is a difference. And if you have or ever had a soulmate cat with you, then you just *know* it, even though you aren't sure how or why you know it.

Let's elaborate on the soulmate. We don't want to go too deep into the concept of what the soul is. Suffice it to say that the soul is the part of you that never dies but carries on through all dimensions and realms and vibrations and even incarnations. The soul is your essence. It's what makes you you, in your purest form. Many books and essays have been written about the soul, the spirit, etc. For the sake of this archetype categorization, and the important purr-pose of the soulmate in your life, here is our explanation:

The soul is the eternal part of you, of us, of everyone in this universal experience. The soul is what carries the spark of consciousness. It has an expression, a uniqueness, a unique fingerprint. It's what carries all memories, all experiences, and all unique gifts that you bring to this world, including your purpose and mission. You are here with a distinct purpose. We'll talk about *your* unique soul purpose, dear human, in a later chapter. But just like you, we cats have a distinct life purpose for the duration of our incarnation. And our soul has a bigger mission that spans over millennia and several lifetimes. So our soul comes with a multitude of experiences, tasks, knowings, and soul contracts.

Yes, we are contracted to you, or our soul is entwined with yours during the duration of your stay in this lifetime and even beyond. It's what brings us together, life after life. When you have a soulmate cat in your life, then you have a companion who has been following you throughout the ages, who has incarnated beside you, with you, and for you over and over again.

All the other cat archetypes can also be reincarnated with you and can have been in your life before. But the soulmate cat is a friend forever. And yes, we know that forever is a big word. So let's just say that your soulmate cat has been with you for eons and he's likely not going anywhere anytime soon. So if you have or had a soulmate cat in your life – and you'll always know – then there is a *very* good chance that he'll come back to you sometime soon and probably again in this lifetime.

How do you know you have a soulmate cat? Well, you just know. We can't explain it in much detail, because it is more a feeling than a checklist. When you are in the presence of that cat, then you just feel at home. You feel cherished, you feel loved, you just want to have him by your side. Always and all the time.

Similar to the supporter, the soulmate will understand you without words. He "gets you". You feel you don't have to explain yourself, you can just *be yourself*. In every sense of the word. You can feel at your absolute worst, but he'll make you feel radiant, whole, and complete. When he is not with you, you miss him. When he is with you, then everything is right in your world. It is just the most miraculous and the most magnificent feeling in the world when your soulmate cat is around you.

There are also other factors at play. The soulmate cat is not just there for your pleasure or for your "feeling whole". No, he actually has a few more important things to do, such as to guide you, when you are looking for the way. Or to nudge you, when you are taking things too slow or not paying attention. Yes, we are talking about showing odd or weird behavior, when he feels that you are not aligned with your values, your truth, and your highest path.

In that sense, the soulmate cat can also be your mirror, your teacher, your muse, your supporter, or even your healer. All of it, some of it, or most of it. The soulmate is a quite "complete" or well-rounded member of our species, and he is always there for you to push you or better to guide you along on your journey.

Let's round this out by saying that your soulmate is of course there with a higher or bigger purpose – because your soul is that part of you, of your experience, that carries your purpose, your passion, your creative forces. So the soulmate cat's task is to remind you of this! Of who you truly are, of what you came here to do, and most of all, of being happy, and being in your love and your ease and your purpose.

Most importantly, your soulmate cat will remind you of being *YOU*, of being happy, of being purposeful, and of being in your power. How? By displaying odd behavior when you are not aligned. By mirroring your emotions, when you are too angry, or too timid, or too stressed out. By being there to show you *where* you are not aligned, by lying in your tight spots (physical spots on your body), or even by clawing you or biting you, if you don't get the memo. In that sense, your soulmate cat is quite a comprehensive character and busybody, but of course, you wouldn't want it any other way. Because you were the one who invited him into your life, so that he could be your trusted friend and companion, but also your guide and barometer, so you can fulfill all your soul contracts and expand and walk your highest soul path. You are the one who forged all the soul contacts with him!

As we cats follow you throughout the ages, the soulmate cat tends to come more often than others because his task is never really complete, and he will add more contracts to his list throughout time. He is truly your best friend and your guide in the long run. He will know when you are about to embark into a new human life journey, and his soul will be right there with you, in the reincarnation room, and ask to be put on the list of souls or companions that you'll encounter during your next incarnation. And yes, make no mistake, that list of soul contracts is long, but your soulmate cat will always make sure that the contracts he shares with you will be loving and caring, and most importantly, of the highest frequency.

To summarize this archetype, the soulmate cat is your best friend and will go through thick and thin with you. You'll just know what he wants and needs, and you'll naturally gravitate towards each other. So you don't have to be afraid of losing him or not recognizing him in his new incarnation, because the Universe – and you two souls – have a way of finding each other again and again.

🐾 THE HEALER

This one is indeed quite magical! He is the epitome of healing and vibrating at the highest levels. He usually comes into your life when you are down and out, or when you are in dire need of healing: either emotionally or physically.

The healer cat will be by your side through any kind of purging, be it old emotional baggage, or burdensome karmic relations, or unresolved life topics. He will be there either supporting you through the process, or instigating the process, or just witnessing it. In reality, he will be working his magic in the background, unbeknownst of his magical ability to change the vibration around you and all your bodies (mental, physical, astral, emotional) and by also changing the frequency in your home.

Yes, they usually don't just work for you. When you have a healer cat, then he is there for all of your world: you, your family members, your home, your relationships, your work situation, etc. He will be working his magic, like a wizard or magician, throughout all areas of your life. He will heal your physical ailments by lying on those of your body parts that need healing. Even the scientific medical world has concurred and conceded that a cat's purring can heal bones and other body structures. So even your medical board has given their blessing for us cats to be around you in crisis situations. And while *all* cats have that magical feat and ability of purring in order to heal you, there is an even higher vibration around the healer cat. He will literally heal your bones, your tissues, your heart and soul, or whatever else needs healing.

Let us clarify the concept of healing at this point: it's not necessarily just mending something that is broken. It is more so a bringing back into balance and alignment, which was not in its highest vibration and alignment before. So the healer cat (like a healer person) will bring back into balance what is off balance. And this goes, as we said before, for your medical issues as much as for your emotional issues, for your relationships with people, for your work – for your entire life.

We want to elaborate more on the concept of balance. From a cat's point of view, life is naturally balanced. We spend lots of time sleeping, and we divide our awake time equally between hunting, feeding, grooming, relaxing, and cultivating social contacts. This includes caring for our young ones and spending time with our siblings, our closest cat friends, and other members of our family, including our human family.

The point is that our awake time is spent by doing many different things. We truly strive for balance in our lives. Anything that you would call a stressful situation, we usually offset it with fun, playing, sleeping, or hanging with our buddies – humans or others. There is not much time factored in a cat's life for things that make up much of a human's life. By saying this, we are not meaning to be disrespectful. But we don't have much space in our lives for what you spend time on: the planning, the worrying, the being in stressed anticipation of how events might (not) unfold. The worrisome handling of family and friend relationships, which are often strained with the should have's, could have's, would have's, or what you think is expected of you. And yes, then there is the job situation, which makes many of our beloved humans very sick or stressed out, or in short, not very happy.

While we do understand – and it's important for us to say this – while we do appreciate and understand that our food and our home and all the amenities that we enjoy when living with you, like treats and toys, are being paid for by you, we can clearly see that you are making certain sacrifices for it. You sacrifice how you spend many hours of your precious lifetime to be able to provide these comforts and amenities for yourself and for us in our home. But we also know that truly we all – humans included – are supposed to live in joy, flow, and ease! Much of what we see or witness firsthand from our humans revolves around stress, around "I *have* to do this, whether I like it or not". Your livelihood and all your amenities have a high price on your sanity, your emotional wellbeing, and even your physical integrity.

Since it is not up to us cats to reshape your society and how things work in the human world, let's just conclude these thoughts by saying that we do appreciate everything you do for us. But we also notice that much of your comfort and luxury comes at a high price for your balance and your soul. Which brings us back to the concept of balance, and how we cats can contribute to making your dutiful and complicated life so much better.

The healer cats literally assess the level of balance needed in your life, and then they'll attune their healing energies to that perceived gap. They will manage to create whatever frequency is currently lacking in your life, and then fill in the gap, or slowly elevate your frequency to guide you to the state you wish to be in. So in that sense, the healer is the balancer, the facilitator, the equilibrium you need to restore *your* natural balance of being. By understanding how we cats balance our day or our beingness, it can give you a better idea of how you can structure your ideal day or your designated "you" time for your highest way of being.

Healer cats come in different forms and expressions. Some just have the magical ability to match and uplevel your frequency. Just by purring and being next to you, they'll "rub off" on you and give you their frequency – so that you and all your bodies can come into balance.

Other healer cats have a more refined form of healing. They are here specifically to heal your heart, or your soul, and even your karmic history. They'll be with you for a certain period of time, helping you go through your life drama, and then help you purge and let go, and go into the new.

Then there is the trauma healer. They go hand in hand with the above emotional and karmic healing, but we mean in this case physical trauma. These cats are fabulous and typically come into your family when you have a lot of physical trauma to go through. This is everything from broken bones to chronic health issues, to the ever prevalent cancer. These specific physical healer cats are phenomenal in detecting even the slightest change in your body, and they will react to it. Either by adjusting their frequency (and their sleeping positions next to you) to the body area that needs healing, or by letting you know that you have an issue there. Many cats have shown their humans physical problems in the making before even the first symptoms appeared. So in that sense, this healer is almost psychic or almost a physical doctor – whichever you prefer to have by your side.

Let us conclude this archetype by adding that many healer cats are also there to help their humans do their healing work. They'll come to you when you start to work with the healing arts. They will be by your side when you increase your adeptness and your abilities in the healing arts. And they will definitely be by your side when you see clients in your home or work on people remotely. These healer cats not only help you actively with your healing work with other people – they'll also heal you in the process. Many human healers report that it's easier to heal others than themselves. That's where the healer cat comes in. He basically becomes a healer's healer! And that's all we have to say about this cat archetype. We love him, and we wouldn't want to be without this fantastic colleague in our midst.

🐾 THE ENERGY WORKER

This is an exquisite one! We'd like to elaborate here a little bit. There are actually two distinct types of energy workers among us cats. The first one is an energy facilitator or energy holder. The second is a bit more difficult to explain, so let's start with the easier one.

The energy facilitator (for lack of a better word) is the one that, when around you, will clear and cleanse energies in your area. He'll energetically cleanse your home, and your family members (humans, cats, dogs), and, of course, he'll cleanse you. This means that he'll literally suck the denser energies out of your field and from your surroundings. By doing so, the energy facilitator will not only suck the "negative" energies out but also put "positive" energies back into the field. So in this sense, he functions much like a power plant or a transformer. Most of this work is really performed within his energy field or his aura, and some of it in his body. This makes him heavier and not as "light" as other cats, but he is quite literally a powerhouse of a cat! They'll lay seemingly lazy or sleepy in the corner, but they are truly working overtime without you even noticing.

Many times, these cats tend to be a bit heavyset, because they have to physically offset the energies they draw to them, but they are nevertheless light when it comes to their personality and their vibration. Their vibratory body is an exquisite machine of delicately interwoven frequency transmitters and cleaners. They can create vortexes and energy fields around you. When an energy facilitator does his job, everyone in the room or the home will benefit from it. They are usually thorough in what they do unless they encounter very dense or darker energies, or when they get worn out by too much overwhelm going on with their humans.

This leads us to the second type of energy workers. As they are a bit more subtle in nature, we'll want to keep it as simple as possible. This energy worker is a pure golden light. We'd like to switch here to the female form, to give them credit where it's due. She is purely magical and golden in nature. She is so etheric that she is almost like a feather. In her company, you'll feel like you're among the elves or the fairies, or other magical creatures. This "energy fairy" is there for her human to help shift into the highest of frequencies! Very often, these elven-like energy being cats are there for humans who are already in a higher version of the Ascension process. They pave the way, so to speak, for their humans to become the highest version of themselves, at every step of the journey. As the human evolves into their higher vibration, so will the cat. And together they create a magical environment for others to thrive.

This cat often comes to people who are quite advanced on their journey, who are healers, lightworkers, starseeds, wayshowers, and aware of their place in history or in the tapestry of life. This cat facilitates their human's spiritual path in a way that no other cat can. Therefore it was important for us to make this distinction for energy worker cats: from the physical shifting of energies as the main task (version 1) to the ethereal shifting of higher vibrations (version 2).

Let's move on to what is similar in both versions: both energy worker cats work in unison with their humans and are very closely interwoven with their human counterparts. They usually know exactly what they are doing, and they are used to being misunderstood in many ways. For the energy facilitator might seem "lazy" to the unknowing human, and the energy fairy might seem "distant" to the uninitiated human eye. In any case, both of these cats are magnificent in their energetic makeup, and unique in the way they can sense and transform energies in their purest form. Both of them come in a very high frequency, and they are automatically, without a flaw or without even thinking twice about it, always and all the time working, raising the frequencies in your home, for their people and for their fellow cats or dogs in the house.

In closing, the energy worker cat is one that is really easy to have around. They don't seem to need much maintenance or special care. They are independent, loving, do their thing, and mind their own business. Some of them tend to seem like loners, but others are very social and are the backbones of the cat group, by filtering out all tension and social mis-interaction and bringing peace and balance to the group as a whole. In that sense, the energy workers are also miracle workers or social workers, in balancing the cat group. But they are also there for their humans! Many of them tend to be cozy and lazy, but make no mistake: they are pure powerhouses and always work their magic in the background. You are truly blessed if you have an energy worker cat in your home.

🐾 THE MIRROR

Let's move on to a more complicated archetype: the mirror. This one is a bit trickier or more elaborate. Let's start by saying that mirrors are some of the most important cat companions for you to have around. Some of the most laborsome, too, but nevertheless very important. Especially with the state of humanity and the world in the aftermath of 2020, we've been in a state of helping our humans out. We could also say we cats have been in the business of helping out our humans for millennia, but it was never as important as it is now!

Humanity is at a stage where you purge and move through *all* of your past life regressions, meaning that everything that has accumulated in the human field for millennia is now coming out so it can be processed once and for all and leave the human field for good. This is the main reason why things in the world seem to be culminating the way they are currently. When you feel you observe more bloodshed, more violence, more trickery, more "bad" things than ever, then you are not incorrect. It's time for all these things to once again bubble up before they can be purged or cleansed. This is one of the main reasons why you – yes you, my dear reader, quite possibly a lightworker, starseed, or soul that is here to help clean the human field – are tasked with so many ingressions and things to purge in your own life. You are here to help humanity let everything go, and start almost fresh. How? We'll get into that later.

Suffice it to say that a mirror cat has a very important place in your life: she will show you – almost mercilessly – where you are not yet aligned with your highest truth. Where you still labor around old wounds from childhood, ancient beliefs that aren't yours, and programming in your physical bodies about your limitations, lack, and misfortunes. This, my friend, is luckily all about to change, or it's changing already as we are speaking.

We have set up the premise that you humans are going through a major purge, and that we cats are here to help humans – and cats and all other species – to evolve into a higher form of being. By being your mirror, your precious cat companion will show you exactly where your stress points, your pressures, your misbeliefs, your old heartaches and emotional wounds, and your core wounds lie. This is meant to be your breakthrough, your aha moment, where you and your travel companion embrace the most wonderful journey you are here to partake in: the journey back to yourself!

Your core wound is usually what you were born with. Not good enough, not rich enough, not pretty enough, not fulfilled, not having luck with relationships, not being in your highest truth (meaning living a life of lies and misconception), not being able to love, not being empathetic, etc. There are numerous core wounds within humanity, but for the purpose of this book, let's pick one of the most common ones. The core belief of not being lovable, of not being worthy, of constantly having to prove yourself. If you came with this core wound or belief, then your whole life will be shaped around this and be a mirror of your beliefs. You might not be fortunate in love matters. You might have money issues, or not getting fairly remunerated for your services. You might have an issue with your looks or with your standing in the world. You'll always encounter situations where other people seem to be favored over you. You'll have a belief that if you were just better looking, or richer, or have a better job title, or live in a fancier home, or have a famous circle of friends, or be more accepted in your workplace, or in your neighborhood... then everything will be fine, and you will be happy. Or if only you could lose those 20 pounds, then you'll be fine. Or if only you could afford that fancy car, then you'll be somebody, and you'll finally be happy.

But deep inside, you already know the answer: if you define your happiness with outside views or looking for your worth in objects, or how other people see or define you, then you'll never be happy.

Yes, happiness is an inside job! You need to find your own happiness inside you. Your self-love. Your self-worth. You being you and the most wonderful thing on the planet. You being in your frequency of love and joy. You being in your innate beautiful and unique soul frequency. You being yourself!

This is where your mirror cat comes in. Most likely she has the same life experience or core wound that you have: not being seen or heard. Having been abandoned in the streets. Having been the only one in the litter that didn't get adopted. Feeling ugly, worthless, not being wanted. By synchronicity, you take heart and adopt this "not worthy" feeling cat. You know what happens? She will mirror your own life circumstances back at you!

She'll feel that she is not entitled to your unconditional love. She'll let other cats mob her. She'll leave the sleeping spot next to you to the other cats because she feels she's not worthy to be in the top spot. She might run and hide when visitors come over because she doesn't dare to show herself. She won't play with the other cats, because she's too self-conscious to get pushed aside, and so she only comes out of her shell at night, when the other cats are asleep, and won't bother her while she plays. And so on...

What this cat does is mirror your own lack of self-worth back to you! So when you see your mirror cat hiding, then go within: where do you hide your light? When you see your mirror cat being mobbed by other cats, then feel in: where do you let people walk all over you, or where do you not stand up for yourself? When you see your mirror cat give way to the other cats, then think of yourself: where do you let others go first and you don't assume your rightful place? Where do you not trust the hand that feeds you, or where do you not believe that the Universe has your back?

The list is endless. Let us give you other examples, for other issues and other mirror cats. An aggressive cat might mirror a person who is angry at the world and lashes out. A timid cat mirrors a person who hides their light and their greatness from the world. A restless cat reflects a person who is nervous, restless, or not at ease. A cat who won't let anyone pet or touch her usually reflects a person who won't let others near them (physically or emotionally). A cat with trust issues reflects a person who doesn't trust other people or doesn't trust life itself. And so on. Even when two cats fight or don't get along, it is usually a reflection of their people who have a rocky relationship, who fight a lot, or who have lost their respect or that "loving feeling" for each other. Yes, dear humans, we cats do pick up any tension between you, and we act accordingly! If we feel that you don't notice how strained your relationship with your partner is, then we'll usually mirror your behavior in cat form. We'll mirror how you "hiss" at each other, how you avoid each other in the home, how you lash out at each other, or how you "growl" at each other.

It's important for us to state that all of what we do when we mirror you, we do out of utter and complete and boundless love for you, our humans! And we do it for different reasons. There are actually two versions of mirror cats. Let's explain the difference.

In version one, the cats consciously mirror your behavior, so you see yourself in them and become aware of your actions and emotional states, and then you can do something about it.

By doing this, we mirror cats fully know that we might get in trouble or that we are being instigators. One cat might knowingly take on the role of the bad guy in the play, chasing the other cats around, fully knowing and accepting that he'll get a bad rep out of it. But he does so in endless love to you, so you'll catch yourself in the act, so to speak, and recognize yourself in his instigatory behavior! And we fully know that you never mean to be the bad guy. But we also know that your human life is full of stress and stressors and things that make you get angry and frustrated and leave you overwhelmed, which then inadvertently makes you lash out at the world.

Oh, the overwhelm we see in our humans! All we want to do is hug you and help you through it. But in many cases, such as the mirror cats, their job is to hold the mirror in front of you, in the hope of you recognizing yourself in them, and then consciously correcting your behavior.

In the second version of this cat, it's more about mirroring your core wound or childhood imprints. In this case, you'll most likely get a cat in your life that comes with the same childhood wound or life topic as you: having been let down early in life, not feeling worthy, not trusting life, being overly sensitive, being overly protective, being overly vain (overgrooming), etc. The list is endless.

Suffice it to say that these cats always come with the highest intentions and the most loving heart. At a soul level, they know exactly what they are in your life for, and the journey they are taking with you. For they are in your life, so that you'll recognize yourself in them, look into your unconscious patterns, your beliefs or disbeliefs, your imprints, your karmic wounds, and then you can start your journey of healing. Just by consciously knowing or recognizing what needs healing, you start the healing process. And however you work through it, your cat is by your side. You can harness their help to go through this! With a timid cat, you can both encourage each other and together learn to show yourself more to the world. With a trust issue cat, every time you see your cat shy away from your hand, it can be a reminder of becoming more trustful yourself – trusting the Universe, trusting other people, trusting someone who holds out their hand to you, etc. This is the journey you are in together, and your cat's behavior – or your cat's progress in becoming more trustful, more peaceful, more at ease – will also be a reflection of your own journey or where you stand. So as you see your cat getting "better" and overcoming their patterns, it is always a wonderful and encouraging reminder of where you stand. In this sense, your mirror cat is your barometer for your moods, emotions, issues, or life topics.

This concludes this oh-so-important representative of our species. They might not be the epitome of a cat (meaning not being in the love and joy frequencies most of the time), but they are more important than ever to have around. They need to be appreciated for all the work that they do, and they have a special place in our hearts.

🐾 THE MUSE

This one is quite literally or almost the opposite of the mirror! The muses are the epitome of a cat: free-spirited, loving, and caring, but very independent. They do whatever they please and are seemingly always at ease with the world, their surroundings, and who they are.

The muse is a magnificent cat. She is usually very much in tune with nature. She will rise with the sun and go with the flow all day long. If not an outdoor cat, then she'll adjust to that indoor environment as well, but she will always be free at heart.

What does the muse do for her human? Well, quite literally inspire them! She will be the epitome of freedom, of free will, of living in joy, harmony, and in tune with nature and with her nature. Yes, that includes bringing home mice and birds, in order to show her human her fierce hunter side. She will stand in all her glory and show you to not be afraid of your shadow side! For we cats understand what we are: nature has made us into a predator of smaller animals. We hunt animals in the wild that have a lower form of consciousness than us. We do appreciate that mice and birds are here for us as prey and food. That being said, many humans wonder why we still hunt, even though we are well-fed. That lies in our nature – the very nature that a muse cat will show and be in tune with when she is out there. To hunt means to hone your skills of smelling, hearing, and seeing. To follow your instincts, to burst out in a sprint and feel the force and the speed of your body while running across the grass. Yes, even the catching of the prey is part of a skill set of hunters and predators that nature – or let's say creation – endowed us with. Are we proud of it? Well, some cats are. They are the ones that live close to their nature and embrace all of who they are.

What humans can learn from that trait in us, and that brings us back to the muse, is to embrace their shadow side. Everybody and every species has them! In this world, in this Universe, there are different forces at play that quite literally "play" with each other. It's how the Universe expands and how everyone who lives in it learns and evolves and grows. If everything were of the purest of light, then there would be stagnation. No growth, no exploration. So the dark side, or let's say the shadow side of beings, including humans and cats, enables us to explore the "other" side of the spectrum of emotions, of being in this body, being in a physical environment. Make no mistake: once you cross over into the higher realms, yes, there will be peace and love and the feeling of bliss and joy. The higher you move up in the dimensions, the more expansive the experience of peace will be. And that is what this planet is moving towards. But in the meantime, we still live in a physical world of opposites, of shadow and light, and this is how the cats and the humans learn and evolve into their higher state of being.

Back to the muse: she is really exquisite. She is usually of a delicate look, and she is fierce and gracious at the same time. She will come to those in the process of moving into a higher state of consciousness. She will then be by your side to show you how to be free and at ease. How to embrace your shadow side and then transgress into a state of limitless love and joy of being in this world, being in this body, and being who you are.

The muse does even more than that. She will also be your guide when it comes to your spiritual endeavors, such as meditation, healing arts, or even the fine arts, such as writing, pottery, making music, or anything that is in the creative spectrum. She will be sitting with you when you write your books or poems. She will be purring by your side when you compose your music or your finest recipes, or your piece of art, whatever the nature of it is.

Yes, the muse is quite literally that: she will inspire you to do what you are here to do, without her seemingly *doing* anything! Because that is exactly what she inspires or teaches you to do. You don't necessarily have to *DO* something in order to be *YOU* or to bring your gifts to the world. Just as she effortlessly shows you how to glide through life, by just being in the moment or by just being fully herself, she teaches you to do the same. To let go and let god, and to just let the writing do itself. Or the painting, or the creating of whatever wonderful thing it is that you bring into the world.

The muse will be by your side also when you go into a new phase of life. She will accompany you through health and sickness, through ups and downs, and through many other phases of your life that are not stagnant and sedentary, but at times seem like upheaval or even trauma. Your muse cat will be there for you, not to physically heal you (like the healer cat) and not to help you carry your emotional burden (like the supporter or soulmate). Instead, the muse will be there to bring you joy and love, and to serve as a beacon of how wonderful life can be, once you clear through the mental and emotional clutter and just allow yourself to be happy.

In that sense, the muse can have crossovers with the joybringer and the teacher – which is to come up – as many of their idiosyncrasies and outer traits seem to overlap. But the difference is that the muse always has one thing that makes her unique: her nonchalance with the world, with circumstances, with you even, or with how she comes across to others. Different from the joybringer (who has this irresistible air of cuteness or amiability around him that makes even the iciest human heart melt), the muse will always be true to herself, do whatever she pleases and thereby can come across as self-absorbed, super-independent, not one wanting to please, to the point of even quirky at times. So while the joybringer will win your heart with his endearing mannerisms, the muse might throw you off by prancing her sovereignty in your face. She is not there to please you! She is there to nudge you and guide you, and to let you know how life is supposed to be lived: by being in the moment and enjoying it to the fullest.

That brings us to the next archetype that has certain similarities but differs in their intent and mainly in their intensity of expressing themselves.

❧ THE TEACHER

This one is a very important member of our species. Not that the others aren't – as a matter of fact, there is no better or higher or more important archetype than the other. All cats are equally participating in this grand experience that you call Earth. But the teacher comes with a certain package. You might call it emotional baggage, or a wealth of wisdom under his wings. He is most likely an old soul and had many incarnations as a cat (or other animal species) on this planet. He is mostly coming from the Earth realm or from the higher realms.

We are not distinguishing between an Earth soul or a starseed soul, as they are all in line with each other. Some souls are born on distant planets and then incarnate here, to bring their wisdom and experience to planet Earth. And others are just born here or around this realm, and then they incarnate in a human or cat body, as they are closely originated from here. And yes, this means not just Earth but also other planets in Earth's vicinity: Mars, Tiamat, Venus, etc. So the starseeds usually come from afar, while the Earth seeds or *true* human souls (if there is such a thing) come from Earth or Earth's vicinity, in this solar system. That is the only distinction. They are all old or can be old souls. They all have experience and wisdom, and high vibrational bodies. The difference is that Earth seeds are well-rooted here on this planet and in this planetary system. They regard it as home and therefore have fewer issues or problems relating to other humans or the structures and the laws and even the physicality of this planet. For this is where they truly first incarnated in their pure soul form.

The starseeds, on the other hand, originated in other planetary systems with different laws, different views of how the world works, different mindsets, and, of course, different bodies. So they have a harder time adjusting to the atmosphere, the people, their auras, the customs, the way of walking, and overall being in a human form. For they come from worlds with different bodies, different physiologies, and different vibratory states. As a result, they come here and struggle with being human, being on this planet, and understanding the human race.

Back to the teacher cat, who is very much connected to the Earth realm and likely an Earth seed. She is a superb member of our species! She usually carries the knowledge of many lifetimes – her own soul's and her lineage's wisdom. She will share this wisdom not only with other cats or dogs in the household but most importantly, with her humans. That is her task, that is why she comes into your life.

How does she do it? Simple: by being herself, and leading by example. By showing you how things "should" be or should be done. While we don't really like the word "should" – it tries to put things into a box – we use it here deliberately, because it paves the way to how humans are going to put themselves out there, once this project Earth goes into the next stages. This means that the teacher cats come to you to prepare you for the future. To help you recognize your old "stuff", your emotional baggage, your core wound, your unhealed and often hidden childhood imprints and programs that run undetected in your body and field, rendering you unable to move forward with your plans or desires.

So how does the teacher do all that? By being by your side. By showing you how you "should" or "could" put yourself out in the world – very much like the muse, thus leading by example. Or by showing you your own unresolved life topics, much like the mirror who comes with the same themes as you or develops the same emotional states. But the difference is that the teacher is above all that! While the mirror cat truly goes through all the troubles and tribulations of your conditions with you – be it unresolved trauma or emotional issues – the teacher will remain above them. She will view your condition from a higher point of view, offering comfort or advice or exemplary living, or even showing you by meowing, scratching, biting, or being "in your face" with something, that you need to change your ways.

In that sense the teachers can be quite strict and sometimes uncomfortable to be around. However, they'll also be lovingly by your side, nudging you to go in the right direction or to even turn around completely, if you must. The teacher is very important to have around, now more than ever, with the state of humanity and the world being more heightened than ever. So we congratulate all teachers for being their sublime selves and being so gentle but strict, so kind but nudging, and so wise but loving with their humans.

We'd like to add that the teacher is just like a human teacher: wise and knowledgeable about life in general, about what it means to be a cat but also what it means to be human. The teacher will always "teach" – it's in her genetic makeup and in her field. She cannot help but always give advice. So this cat might push or nudge you more than other cats. She really wants you to understand her teachings or what she is in your life for. She will also be kind and gentle and lend a shoulder to cry on – or a soft coat for you to stroke and cuddle in that respect. She will always be there for you and always catch you when you fall. But make no mistake, she will also enforce her teaching agenda, and she will oversee it with an iron fist – or a sharp claw. *(The cats are smiling – they love it when they use a human play on words).*

When you have a teacher cat by your side, your growth is almost guaranteed and built-in! So you can be happy and hopeful that you'll make it to the next grade, or your next level of beingness. The teacher cat will make sure that you graduate, ideally with honors. Like any good tutor, she will be on your butt about learning, about doing your due diligence in whatever matter she assists you with. Many times it is connected with your personal growth on an emotional but also an energetic level. Sometimes it even has to do with you being or becoming a teacher yourself. When you become a coach or spiritual teacher, then most likely you'll need a good life coach by your side. In this case, you'll get your very own spiritual personal cat coach. She will teach you the zen moments in life as much as she will teach you how to handle your students. With proper love and care, but also with an iron claw, to make sure they'll reach their class goal and go over the finish line, always in line with what their souls are contracted to do here.

So rest assured, with a cat teacher by your side, you will always reach your class goals, or in this case, your spiritual graduation. And that's all we want to share about this wonderful cat species for today and for this classroom.

🐾 THE PROTECTOR

The next archetype is the protector. And what a strong representative he is! While protection seems like a feat that dogs would provide for humans, there are also some protectors in our species. We'll elaborate on the different kinds of protection they provide in a minute. Upfront, we would like to point out that humans are generally perfectly capable of protecting themselves – in an energetic manner, at least. But as always, we are glad to be of service and to give our humans some extra protection where needed. Say, you are a healer or energy worker or some kind of intuitive, or "just" an empath in everyday life. You will get in contact with spirits or darker energies (we prefer to say denser or lower energies), and some of you are not aware that you are getting in touch with these entities or energies. So that is where we cats step in.

Cats can, as commonly acknowledged, perfectly see or feel entities and energies in different dimensions – be they lower or higher. So we'll sense the energy attacking you, and we can step in before they get too strong. The way the protector will do that is either physically placing himself next to you or in the area where you are most vulnerable. That might be your throat chakra or heart chakra, or any other body part that you use for your healings or for your work. The protector cat will then literally throw a protective energy field around you, and thus fend off or limit the access the lower entity has over you. So the energy protector cat is not necessarily "stronger" than you but has almost seismic qualities in detecting destructive or lower energies before even the most sensitive human energy worker can sense them.

The second form of protection is more of an Earthly nature. These cats will follow their humans around, much like dogs, and will try to help you through the tougher moments in life. That could be some kind of emotional drama, where the protector cat won't leave your side, just like the lover or supporter. Or, he'll quite literally be glued to your side when you go through a tough work project or training program, or anything that comes through your computer, where the protector will sit, lie, or rest against you, in order to physically (and emotionally) guide you through the process or situation.

The protector will also growl or hiss at people who he feels bother you or aren't good for you. This is the cat that will literally push a visitor off the couch, by squeezing between you and the visitor, thus keeping him from touching you or getting too close to you. He has also been known to chase a new romantic partner out of the bed of "his" human because he (the cat) feels the new partner hasn't proven himself enough yet to be worthy.

The protector is not afraid of playing the role of the bad guy. Just like a good guard dog, it is his job to help you out and to protect you from harm! That can include new people, new partners, new business partners, or any other person that comes into your life. The protector cat takes his job very seriously, and while he might not bite visitors or bark at them like a dog, he will be in the room supervising the situation, ready to step in if he thinks you need help or protection.

This one is, in terms of quantity, the rarest of the cat archetypes, but nevertheless, he is an important member of the cat family – and of your family, if you'll let him. So when do you get a protector cat in your life? Whenever you feel vulnerable, whenever you embark on a new journey in your life, and whenever you need energetic protection.

Let's go back to the energetic protectors for a moment. These cats have an incredibly strong aura. They have literally a shield around them, which they can extend to include their humans and even other cats. You feel strangely safe in his presence, and you feel you can let your guard down. So in this sense, he is a very reassuring companion to have by your side and someone who will guide you on your soul's journey for many years to come. Your protector cat will be protecting you for life!

At this point, we'd like to talk about a commonly asked question: can a cat's archetype or task change over the course of time? The answer is yes. It's not likely that they'll make a 180° turn and go from, say, serious teacher to funny joybringer. But yes, a cat's purr-pose can shift over time, much like a human's can. And we are never saying that any cat is always just one particular archetype. Some cats have more than one task or more than one characteristic expression. And then they can shift in the course of their life, as needed by their human, and as their soul grows and shifts.

Let's say a cat has the expressions of a healer, an energy worker, and also a lover. In most cases, there is one predominant archetype. For the purpose of this example, let's say the cat is a healer in the first part of his life. He is there to heal his human from a traumatic experience, and his healing frequencies are really high. He is also a lover, but in this first stage, his main job is to be a healer for his person. Then, say, a few years later, the person has overcome their ailment through finding energy healing and alternative treatments, and then pursues a career in the healing arts, to help others with similar problems. At this stage, the healer cat might move into becoming more of an energy worker, by holding the energies around his person while they are doing their healing work. And then, years later, the cat might shift more into the lover mode, as he is growing older and stepping back – retiring from the hard work, so to speak – and then living his older years with the very easy and noble task of "just" being the lover cat that his person needs. So in this sense, a cat's work life can be as diverse and fulfilling as a human's career over the years.

This was only part of the shifting of purr-poses, and we'll touch more on it later. The point is that a cat can have more than one purpose and they can shift and change and adapt a bit, according to individual life circumstances and their unique soul's journey.

Going back to the protector, they truly are a very strong personality group, and likely to be your protector for life once they have adopted you as their charge and designated person. This makes them unique and quite special to have around you, not only in times of crises and need but also in your overall life. Who wouldn't want a little protection of their energies and their aura, in these times of changes and vibratory shifting?

🐾 THE STARSEED

This one is a special archetype for anyone reading this who is a starseed. Yes, we are actually talking about your star brother or sister cat! You've always suspected that your cat is not from this world, and here we are, filling you in.

This representative is inherent in many cats, and certainly true of the energy workers, healers, and muses. But we'd like to give it some more depth and exploration. The starseed is a special kind of energy worker that is directly related to your star family. They are of course always here with us in spirit. As we have already touched upon, we cats have been seeded here from the star nations of Lyra, predominantly, but some of us also have roots that go to the Pleiades or Sirius, and some even further to Andromeda and other galaxies.

The starseed cat is a truly magnificent companion. While you as a starseed (and most likely you are one, as you are reading this book) are on your journey of discovering who you are, where your soul comes from, and how to embrace your starseed mission – know that your starseed cat companion will be by your side. Most likely, he will be of your own star lineage and cosmic blueprint.

Whether you are Sirian, Lyran, Andromedan, Pleiadian, Arcturian, or any other starseed, you will always have the right cat in your life. The reason or the importance of their close companionship with you is simple: to be by your side when you awaken to your starseed self. To help you awaken your starseed powers or ignite your starseed mission. To be an example of who you are. And most importantly, to hone you in and activate your frequency as a starseed on Earth. As you embark on this journey of finding your way home to your roots, your cat will help you attune to your unique starseed frequency.

Let's explain a bit further. Each star nation or species has its unique frequency and energy patterns. The Lyrans, be they lion beings or tiger beings, or any other cat beings, all vibrate on a certain frequency, like an energetic or vibratory fingerprint. So do the different Sirian tribes, be it the aquatics or the feline species, or the canine species or the equestrians; or any of the ones that most resemble the humans on Earth. They all have their distinct frequency. So do the Pleidian tribes, and the different Arcturian cultures, and so on.

While every star nation or species has its distinct frequency, all of these patterns are interwoven on a universal level. Quite frankly, all of these patterns are needed for completing the Ascension process on Earth and for this universal experience to evolve to the next level. So while all the patterns are important and needed, they are strengthened as more souls are connecting to their starseed species blueprint, and therefore the patterns get stronger and more pronounced.

To put it more simply: as the Lyran starseeds align with their Lyran soul essence, and the Sirian starseeds realign with their Sirian blueprint and soul essence, they are coming together in more oneness as a soul family, and thus contributing to the completion of the Ascension cycle.

So if you have a starseed cat, then you are truly on your way to becoming a master of your experience! Let's say a human has a very strong expression of being Lyran, and the soul's contracts are playing out for that soul to awaken to their true Lyran-ness, then it's likely that this person will get a Lyran starseed cat in their life for that specific part of the journey. This Lyran starseed cat will then do everything in their power and everything they need to wake the person up to their true form.

That includes expressing behavioral distortions or being "problematic", so that the person is being pushed out of their comfort zone and into the new realms where they are supposed to be. Say a human Lyran starseed's soul path is to become a healer or animal communicator. Their Lyran cat will do anything to push them beyond their limits of comprehension and what would be in the normal spectrum of cat behavior. Consequently, their person is "forced" to look into new ways of dealing with this alarming cat behavior: say dabbling in new healing arts, or learning animal communication, or learning to connect with their spirit guides for help. And boom, that is where their Lyran star family will come in and start communicating, introducing the person to their starseed roots and encouraging them to embrace their gifts and powers. The energy will then shift around the person, and aided by the cat's strong Lyran soul essence energy, the Lyran activations and energy patterns can come in and strengthen the person's Lyran energy field. In other words, the person will become fully activated to their starseed powers and mission, and their soul essence blueprints will be fully established, for their part in the overall awakening of the planet.

This is in short the task of the starseed cat: to awaken their human to their supernatural-ness, their innate powers, and their starseed mission. And, furthermore, to help with the necessary healings, activations, and energy attunements for their soul blueprint to become fully activated.

The starseed cats also come with other tasks, but as we mentioned earlier, a cat's tasks and archetypal features can overlap, and the starseed cat is becoming more prevalent in these times of awakening. They really are magnificent and are so great to have around! Their humans are truly blessed when the starseed cats arrive and get activated and turn the energies in the home into a pure field of love, joy, potential – and of course, purpose.

So we are concluding this chapter about archetypes with the last one that rounds this categorization out:

🐾 THE REBEL

This one has a lot of power and clout in the cat world. They are the ones that rouse up the cat group or are the aggressive cats that bully the others. They are the ones that tear up your furniture or claw you at will. They are the ones that – in short – cause all the problems, or what humans generally call behavioral problems. However, it is important to know that these cats are wonderful souls with a specific one-track task: to elicit change in their human's life!

Yes, it is really not that much about themselves, as people commonly think. It is about challenging the status quo, challenging the existing structures, and pushing their human to their breaking point. What is the purpose of this, you might ask? Well, change is always the chance to let something better come into your life; in this case, in the life of both the cat *and* the human family.

Mostly, you find this archetype in homes where humans go through challenging times. Where they find themselves stuck in their old ways, or where they are unwilling to go with the flow of life or the journey that their soul has planned for them before birth. Many people resist change. They are comfortable in what they know, even if the circumstances are not ideal, or even if their soul is suffering. They'd rather stay in the difficult waters they know than move into smoother waters which they are not familiar with. We are not putting any blame or value judgment on our beloved humans. But we are merely pointing out that humans are sometimes hard to convince that change can be good for them. That moving into a new form of being, or a new job, or a new way of thinking, or into a new phase of life is not only good but necessary. It's the only way to evolve and make progress. Remember, humans *are* here to create. To create a life full of wonder and experiences that make you grow as a soul and as part of the overall experience.

We cats are "in" on your journey, and are actually an essential part of it. So in the case of a human resisting change and not willing to move forward – be it with their inward or outward life journey – then this instigator or rebel cat comes in like a whirlwind and shakes up their very foundation. This cat will start peeing or marking in the house, leaving unmistakable clues as to why or what he is pointing out... unmistakable for cats, but not always understood by their respective humans. In any case, the rebel cat will gladly take on the role of the bad guy and rouse up both the entire cat group *and* the human family, in his quest to shake up their humans, so they'll step up and *change* something in their life.

How does this work exactly? For example, let's say the rebel cat notices that his human is not aligned with her true values. Let's say the person works in a job where services are rendered that her soul is not happy with and that she cannot truly stand behind anymore. The person might have been at this job for 20+ years and sees early retirement coming in 5 years. So she will most likely *not* contemplate leaving the company to find something better, or more suitable somewhere else. Her thinking mind will assess that 5 more years will be fine, to just tide her over, to just keep getting that salary and all the benefits, and *then*, in 5 years, she will finally be free to do what she loves. That is seen from a human perspective, and totally fine from the thinking mind.

But the heart – oh, the heart and soul of the person, which is really truly who she is – will suffer in silence! She will feel guilt over working for a company whose values she can't share anymore. She will feel bad about selling a product that she feels is morally not "good" for people anymore. She will literally internalize all that guilt and shame, and all these dense emotions will trickle deeper into her field and literally form an ulcer or a growth in her body. That is, if no one interferes, by shaking her up and telling her to *not* settle for the comfortable but painful 5 more years at an impossible company but to go for what her heart and soul tell her to do. This might be a new job at a better-suited company, or even doing something for herself. In any case, it would be leaving the known for the unknown, but where her heart would feel so much better in the end.

So where does the cat come in? Well, the cat will either come into your life at that point and/or just not fit in. He will make trouble among the other cats, pick fights, and bully. Or the cat might be rowdy and break stuff, or scratch and bite you, with an over-aggressive demeanor. Or he might – and that is the highest and last escalation – start eliminating around the house. This stage is the most drastic one, and you definitely need to pay attention to it! What does the cat want to say with it? Mainly: "Wake up, my human! You are not happy! You are yelling and growling at people because you are angry at the world. You are breaking stuff in your life because you cannot take it anymore. You are restless, unsettled, and cranky with the world. You have too much internal pressure (signified by the peeing), or you feel like pooping on everyone's parade (we know what that signifies)." The cat might pee in your shoes in the morning to reflect *your* pressure when you have to leave the house to go to your job. Or the cat might pee in front of your bathroom mirror, where *you* usually stand to get ready for work while dreading the very idea of going there. So the cat, in other words, will do everything and anything to draw attention and wake you up to the fact that *you* are not happy with your life.

The best way to go within is to pay attention to *where* the over-the-top behavior takes place. This gives you a good indication of what is "wrong" with you, so to speak. Does the cat mark in your bedroom? Then that's where your pressure is. Does the cat's weird behavior center around the kitchen or overeating? Then you are likely an emotional stress eater. Does the cat fight with the others? Then the cat shows you your own anger or frustration with the world. It's all connected and it's beautifully orchestrated by your rebel cat, the way he shows you where your pressure points or personal issues lie.

The rebel is really quite misunderstood. Of course, he doesn't *like* to be the bad guy or go down in history as the difficult cat. But he usually comes with quite a robust nature, and he can handle the pressure. He has a good sense of self and what's right, and of his important task and mission. He also knows he fights for a good cause. Just like a human rebel, the rebel cat will just *know* that he is right and that he needs to do what he needs to do, to accomplish his mission.

In that sense, he is a wonderful companion to have and so very important to humans, especially at this point in time, where many humans are going through profound changes – not only in their outer life but also in their inner world. The rebel cat will be there for you *through thick and thin,* and to the bitter end. That means he will see his cause through until it is resolved or finished from his standpoint! That's why there are cats that just won't change their instigatory ways, despite all the attempts of cat therapists or vets or animal communicators trying to solve the problem or making the cat change his behavior. But the rebel cats will plainly *not* concede until their humans not only see but resolve their own personal issues, at least to the point of taking all the right steps to a better way of doing things.

You might ask, what is the difference to the teacher cat? It's really in the intensity of the cat's behavior. While the teacher is usually coming from a higher perspective and has the soul presence of a – well – teacher, with a formal attitude and a sharp wit, the rebel comes from a deep passion and *knowing* that he is fighting for the right cause. While a teacher is pointing things out and can also drop the issue when their human is not taking the hint, the rebel will *not* concede until the human makes the necessary changes. That is the main difference. The rebel does not come from the higher perspective but is the hands-on revolutionary with the gun and the motorcycle, just passionately living his cause.

It should be noted that rebel cats are – deep inside – very loving, very loyal, and very much connected with their humans and the other cats that they seemingly despise or fight against. Matter of fact, the rebel is so entwined with their human that he is ususally extremely dear to their person's heart, and it's therefore especially heartbreaking to the human that this cat is "not falling in line". This, in turn, makes his behavior and his cause even more impactful.

Let's conclude this archetype by saying that the rebel is a very important member of the team, and he always deserves to be heard and seen and to have that spot close to your heart.

Now that we have elaborated on all the respective members of our species, where do we go from here? Well, let's talk about you, the human, now. We cats have taken up much space in the book so far, but this book is not just all about cats... but about you as well, dear reader. We are so very fond of you, and we'll have you in the center stage in the chapters to come.

9

WHAT YOUR PURPOSE IS ALL ABOUT

The human concept of purpose is – as we already pointed out – not flawed but has been distorted in these last 20 or so years. We don't want to put a time stamp on here. But ever since the liberation of people from "work" to more "play", there has been a shift in what people call their purpose or the meaning of life. For many centuries, it was more about surviving and doing as best as possible in the human world. But lately, there has been more emphasis on having fun while doing so! On being yourself and expressing yourself in this unique human body, with these unique human abilities, on this unique and wonderful blue planet. So far, so good.

We have already talked about what the meaning of life truly is, from a higher perspective in the higher realms. You come here to create, to bring your essence here, and to create a truly magnificent life. So in that sense, your mere being here is already fulfilling your purpose. This might seem too simple a concept for many people, so let us elaborate.

Your being in human form is already a miracle and proof of your power as a soul. Imagine pressing yourself from a big, miraculous, high-vibrational light being, into a small physical vessel. This in itself is marvelous. Now imagine your light being talking to your human brain in many different facets. Make no mistake: you are *not* your body or your human brain. These are merely vessels for the beautiful, wonderful soul being that you are, so you can come and serve here on this physical plane.

Cats teach you to be in your highest expression

This is where the cats come in. We came here in service (and we are saying this humbly and proudly at the same time). We are here both in service to self *and* others. Much like humans, we come here to play and have fun, and experience life to the fullest. And this is our contribution to the world of humans: to show you and teach you to do the same, specifically how to be the highest and the truest expression of yourself in a human form. So in the same way that the cats are living their truth by being who they are (lazy or active, quiet or loud, gentle or passionate, etc.), this is a reminder for your soul, to be yourself as well.

What does that mean, exactly? Well, the humans come in all different personalities or archetypes, just like us. You, too, are different in your expression and the essence of who you are. Some humans come with the purpose of creating things physically (like phones or cars) and help advance society technologically. Some people's purpose is to provide structure (like building homes or roads or devising schools or administrative systems). Some people come as rebels, dreamers, or visionaries, propelling humanity forward with their ideas, while others come with the mere and very important task of being lovers, or community workers, or providing emotional support for people. Others are bringing joy (much like the feline joybringers), and others are the teachers and coaches in the human world. So in short, the humans can be categorized much like we are, but this is not the content of this chapter. We more so wanted to talk about the vibrational alignment that is taking place on this planet right now, and your place in it.

The human experience is like no other. Many humans are now born with the capability of shifting energies around themselves and others. The new children – some call them crystal children – are coming in at an extremely high frequency. They are aligned with their joy frequency and they are very much in tune with their true nature, and with what they are here to do. Which is, quite simply, to make the world a better place by infusing their joy frequency into the experience.

That's what some would say is the actual purpose of the human experience right now: increasing the joy frequency or the vibration of the human field and the planet as a whole. And as we already established, we cats are pure masters in doing this! Not just the joybringers, no, *all* cats have the remarkable capability of raising the frequency around you, in your house, in your bed, in your study, in your entire home and around your family. We are very much the tuning forks for your experience. In that sense, we are at the forefront of elevating the frequencies on the planet, and we are helping to usher in that new era of a vibrationally higher field on planet Earth, or what some call the Ascension, or what some call the New Earth.

Creating the greatest vibratory experience

So we've established that the joint human purpose is much like the joint cat purpose. It might surprise you that the humans are *not* here to achieve the greatest of advancements, like perfecting rocket science or pushing technology further. Although this is all part of human progress and part of your experience, but the underlying truth is that you are not that much different from us cats. You are a soul in a human body, and you are here to experience the greatest love and joy and fun in creating a vibratory experience for all your senses, that you can possibly muster. This is your true achievement and your true mastery: be yourself in all your facets. Live. Love. Laugh. Be happy. Be the greatest and best vibratory being that you can be. That is your greatest purpose, if you will, and your greatest achievement that you can contribute to humanity.

We can hear your questions arising, and mainly this one: but how can I be such a great vibratory person in an experience with so much – perceived – suffering and hardship? Well, this is the question that humanity keeps asking, and we can shed a bit of light on that. It might be something you've already heard, or it might be new to you. This is the life that you chose. This is the body you chose. This is the family and place and time you chose. To come here and to be the best that you can be in these circumstances. This is the highest you can contribute right now to the planet and this Earth experience as is.

There are multiple other humans out there that are vibing with you, and together, you will make a change. Together, you will make peace. Together, you will create happiness and lasting love and a great experience for all of you, or for all of us. The key really is the *ALL*. You are not alone. You are not solely responsible for healing the planet or curing humanity. You are a fraction – and a wonderful and very necessary fraction – of the experience, of the whole. You are here to contribute your wonderful piece of the puzzle. And you are very much needed for that on the whole. But that's it! You are not here to fix it all. So if you have that need in your field, in your mind, in your heart, that you need to sacrifice your life or yourself or your happiness for the whole – don't! You are not here to suffer along with others, or for the sake of others, or to make someone else feel better. You are here to be the greatest and the best version of yourself. And you are here to lead by example.

By being yourself, you inspire others

Yes, we said it: you being *YOU* becomes a beacon of hope for others. You doing well and creating your best life becomes an example for others to do the same. You being in your highest vibratory state – meaning living a life in love, joy, success, and other great things – becomes a beacon for others to do the same. They'll ask you how you do it, or how you did it. And the best and simplest answer you can give them is: I am leading a life of purpose and joy and love. That is mainly it. And by saying it, you are creating it!

So don't be upset that you might not "be there" yet. That you might not have reached the pinnacle of your career or achievements yet that you set out to do. For you are on your best way to it. There is nothing wrong, by the way, in setting goals for yourself, or wanting to achieve something, or wanting career success, or wanting to make a big change with your work. We are not saying to never want to "change" things in this world. But be aware that it is a joint venture, so to speak, that you are not alone responsible, and that you are not "failing" if these goals don't come in a certain period of time. It is your human mind that is creating or not creating these desired circumstances, and it's not you failing, but your goals may simply not be aligned with your current vibration.

It's really all about the journey. Yes, we know that for humans, they want to arrive and achieve, but the journey is what counts more than the end goal. So try and do your best to really enjoy your journey. It's what you do day in and day out. And wouldn't it be a shame to *not* enjoy your everyday life, in the search or yearning for the day in the distant future that you'll be happy *after* you achieve your goal? Wouldn't it be better to enjoy *every single* day in the meantime?

We, the cats, are coming through again, saying: we are here to help you with that, dear humans! Yes, we have actually mastered the craft of "enjoying every day to the fullest". We are your greatest examples and greatest inspiration to align yourself every day to enjoy your day. Enjoy your daily achievements. Enjoy your daily tasks. We cats do. And so can you.

So your goal should really be the *far* goal, as in the finish line in a very long vacation, if that is a better word than journey. Just see this lifetime here as a vacation on Earth and you are to enjoy it to the fullest. See your goal as being the last day of your vacation, before you leave the fun place to go home. But let's dial back and go a little more into galactic history and how this grand experiment came about.

10

YOUR GALACTIC FELINE ORIGINS

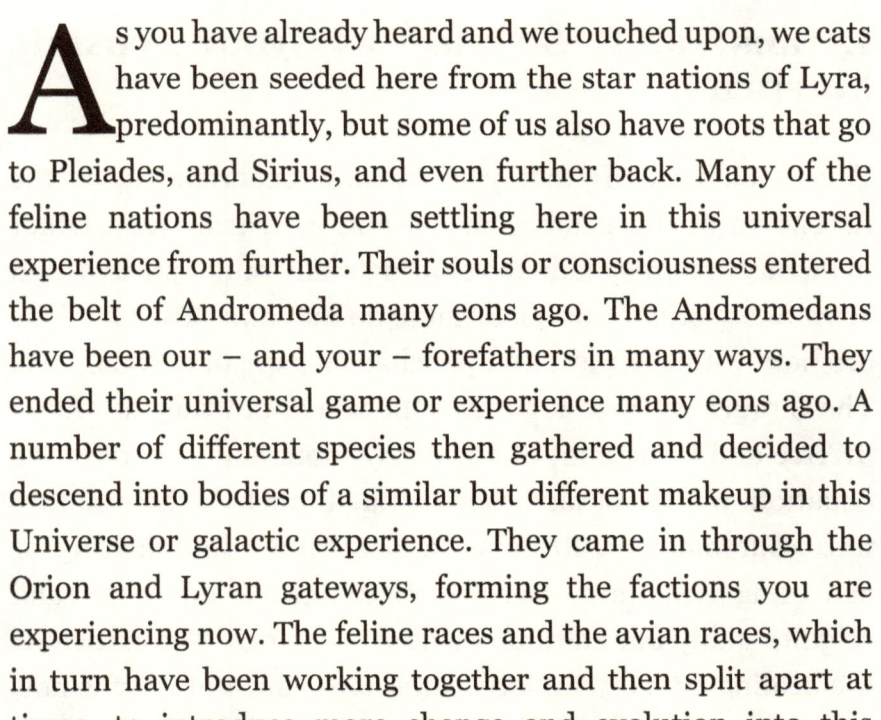

As you have already heard and we touched upon, we cats have been seeded here from the star nations of Lyra, predominantly, but some of us also have roots that go to Pleiades, and Sirius, and even further back. Many of the feline nations have been settling here in this universal experience from further. Their souls or consciousness entered the belt of Andromeda many eons ago. The Andromedans have been our – and your – forefathers in many ways. They ended their universal game or experience many eons ago. A number of different species then gathered and decided to descend into bodies of a similar but different makeup in this Universe or galactic experience. They came in through the Orion and Lyran gateways, forming the factions you are experiencing now. The feline races and the avian races, which in turn have been working together and then split apart at times, to introduce more change and evolution into this universal experience. The Orions became what is now known as the reptilian races, while the Lyrans are all descendants of the feline races of Andromeda. The felines have introduced their love and joy nature into this region, while the avians brought their strong will and their mission for change.

This resulted in battles for territory and became fiercer with time when some factions broke off from the Source connection and started to change the rules of this universal experience. They then became foes of the elders of the game and the feline-descendant races, and that's when the wooing of souls began in certain parts of the Universe.

Lyrans and Sirians as your cosmic blueprint

This is all part of what you are now experiencing as the Ascension of the planets, of the entire solar system. Other planetary systems made the shifting many millennia ago, and are now assisting your quadrant to do the same. The Pleidians are here with their gift and penchant for unconditional love. The Sirians are here for much the same, but they are more diverse and bring a lot of ancient wisdom and culture to the equation. Matter of fact, they instilled much of their culture into your older civilizations, and are now illuminating or activating their starseeds on Earth to uncover and guard and reignite many old cultural wisdom teachings. These include the healing arts, crystal lore, water lore, much of what is now called astrology and other higher forms of working with planetary alignments, old artifacts and high-vibrational places around the Earth that are being reawakened to their old function of power grids, power knots and helping to shift the planetary alignments into a higher form of being.

And then there are the Lyrans... our beloved Lyrans. They are practically the forefathers of us cats, and much of their DNA has been fused into the human genome when the current human experience started about 200,000 years ago. The Lyran DNA was carefully fused and drafted into the DNA of the humans that had dwelled on this blue planet for a long time. You were not genetically enhanced, but it was a long process of using the human genome to make the leap of evolution possible. It was then decided to also fuse other "alien" DNA into these humans, to make them immortal, multi-dimensional, and almost divine-like, like a divine blueprint in a physical form. These beings were truly magnificent in their original form, and many of their souls are now revered as ascended masters. These are the original humans! Yes, this is who you are modeled after and what you have in your DNA. You are no different in your makeup than Yeshua, Mary, Isis, and all the other ascended masters that you are aligning yourself with as a species.

Humans as peacebringers for the galaxy

What's different now, or why did you fall from grace? Your DNA was eventually modified into something even more complex, to add even more evolution into the picture and also to bring some of the other species into this evolutionary state, in an effort to bring peace to the factions that were wrestling for power in these parts of the Universe. To settle the differences, humans were infused with other species' DNA strings, to bring human evolution to an even higher form.

Eventually, this "other" side got a stronger hold over human evolution, and some transgressions were made. The human project didn't get out of hand, but the experience got denser. The lighter forces kept to their oath of not interfering with the process any more than they already had, while the darker forces took the project further. Thus the planet was pushed more into the 3D form than it needed to be, and the true awakening of humanity became a re-awakening after going through a long dark night of the soul.

We are now at the point where the lighter forces are on the upswing, and the darker forces are being ushered out of this experience. In order to not shock the fragile human minds of those who are still completely in the dark about who they truly are as a species, this awakening process has been going slower than some of your awakened people would wish for. It will all be smoothed out in time, and the agenda of the light is strong and on track. In a not-so-distant future, you will live to see the day when the 5D field will so strongly overlap the 3D field that it almost won't be there anymore. Your experience will shift and change gradually so that all humans can adapt to the process. In the following chapters, we will delve deeper into the blueprint of the planet's future evolution and how humans and cats will support this great awakening.

THE CAT SECRET

11

THE NEW YOU

We want to make it exciting and aspiring for you to get into this great state that we cats are already in, without thinking that there are things you have to do to "get there", to this life of love and joy and purpose. For it is really easy and simple to do, and remember, it's part of the vacation fun, not a far-distant goal in the future.

So for a moment, let's revisit your cat's purr-pose in your life. At this point, we want you to take a day or so out of your busy schedule, to tap and feel into your cats, to truly understand what they are in your life for and what they are here to do for you. As you have read all the different cat archetypes, you probably got a pretty good feeling for who your cat is. If you haven't pieced it together yet, then don't worry, we'll help you with that!

Feeling into your cat

Here's an easy exercise to feel in and tap into your cat:

Take a few moments of quiet in your day. Sit down next to your cat or where you can physically feel your cat close to you. Close your eyes, breathe deeply, and try to let go of your thoughts as much as possible. If you are already good at meditation, then go into your meditative state. If you are new to the practice, don't worry. Just take a few minutes to breathe, keep your eyes closed, and try to not overthink the process. Then imagine your cat with your inner vision. Picture your cat coming in and sitting in front of you. Or if your cat lies next to you, place your hand over your cat, so you can physically make contact.

Then conjure up the picture of your cat talking to you. This is a telepathic contact, mind you, for all animals communicate telepathically with each other and also with you. So then either ask your cat what his or her task is with you or ask them to show you. You might get a feeling, or a knowing, or a picture in your inner eye. Just trust your feeling. Trust your intuition. Trust your inner knowing. This is not a contest or rocket science. It is just a feeling into what you already know deep down inside.

The answer should come to you easily. If not, then re-read the sections of the cat archetypes to dig deeper into the topic.

We don't want to go into too much detail here of the "feeling in". We just want to make the process easier for you. Once you have a good idea of what your cat does for you, then you can take the next step: realize where you (or your cat) don't seem aligned or don't seem to have the best life that you are desiring. Where are your weak spots? Where do you feel you are *not* living your best life?

Are you always second-guessing yourself and your life? Do you live according to your own rules or someone else's? Where do you feel you are out of line with your values, your inner compass, and your heart's desires? This is where your wonderful, beautiful cat companion comes in. Whatever their actions are, or however they are "nudging" you with out-of-ordinary behavior, this is where you need your most healing or aligning.

When it comes to your alignment, know that your cat will always be your guide and show you the way! So when you have a cat that displays a heightened or out-of-the-box behavior, then this is the spot or the area you want to work on most. Say your cat does a lot of restless pacing or meowing. This is your topic to look into yourself: where are you restless or not happy in your life? If your cat is aggressive towards you or other cats: where are you angry or attacking others or opposing life circumstances? If your cat is hiding under the bed: where are you hiding from the world? If your cat gets bullied: where do you let others walk all over you? If your cat doesn't like visitors or doesn't want to be touched: where are you not letting people come close to you? Etc.

We do not want to go into all the modes of weird or alarming cat behavior. That is for another time and another book. We just wanted to set the stage for what comes next: overcoming your pattern and embracing who you truly are.

Finding the way back to yourself

The New You is a concept that has often been used by humans in their quest for self-help or self-actualization or other buzzwords. What it really means, though, is to be yourself. Not the distorted or old version of yourself that is running on societal programs and childhood imprints. The New You is also not some version of you that you need to achieve, or strive for, or artificially create with mantras and vision boards. The New You, in the newer sense of the word, as we are going into the New Earth frequencies, is simply a way back to yourself. The way you were when you were *really* young, the exception being if the distortions came with you into this lifetime, in the form of soul contracts and past karma.

The imprinting we are talking about usually starts in the first weeks after the baby (or the kitten) is born. That is when we start taking in emotions and vibrations from our environment. We are literally being coached or guided by our environment into feelings of fear, forlornness, starving for love, not having enough, not being good enough, not being worthy, not being loved, etc. Even when a child is born into circumstances that seem really good and loving and perfect, there can still be some imprinting taking place. For example, if the parents are fighting over the perfect child-rearing methods, or if the kid is being overprotected. These children are getting imprints of fighting *(Over me? I must have done something wrong)*, or being too much in the spotlight *(I have a lot of responsibility to be the perfect child)*, etc. Most of this imprinting is taking place for humans under the age of 7 years old. Most imprinting for cats is done in the first 7 weeks. So this is where our trust and core beliefs are being shaped for us, which then shape our journey in this lifetime.

But let's dial it back and begin with conception. Contrary to popular belief, the soul does not enter the physical body or fetus at conception. This is purely a physical phenomenon that takes place in the body. As the fetus grows, the soul starts to come in. Usually at a few weeks old, but it can also be older, at 2-3 months or so. It all depends on the soul's choices.

Why are we mentioning this? We are talking about the journey of the soul, and soul contracts being made when a soul decides to reincarnate into a physical body. We are talking about humans *and* cats now, and all other highly evolved beings on planet Earth. So let's elaborate. As the soul comes into the physical realm, things change and shift. As the soul settles into the body, and the silver cord is being woven and strengthened, there are contracts and agreements in place regarding what the soul is here in this lifetime to do. This is the same process for cats and humans. As the time progresses, the soul contracts start to play out. So it really starts as early as being in the womb.

We are all here with a divine purpose and soul mission. Your purpose is – as explained earlier – wonderfully interwoven into your soul's plan for this incarnation. The purpose will play out, no matter what! Just know that you can *never* get your purpose wrong. No matter which turns you take in life, you will always get back on track, or land on your feet, to use a comparison from the cat realm.

We cats are the same in that respect: we can never get our purr-pose wrong. When we are born, we will *always* get paired or connected with the cats and the humans that we are supposed to be with. The Universe and this system of reincarnation are so divinely guided and orchestrated, that you can *never* get the wrong cat in your life. It is physically and metaphysically impossible. So lean back and rest assured that all the cats in your life are exactly here as they need to be. The same goes for their issues and behavioral patterns, which are all part of their purr-pose.

It's about your inner, not your outer world

Going back to the New You: it's a concept that humans have been talking about since the dawn of the self-help books and self-actualization movement. It has been used for all kinds of processes, much for your outer processes, meaning new looks, new hairdos, new clothing, as well as new jobs, new job titles, new cars, new apartments, better part of town, etc. Much of the New You, however, is not in the outer world or in your appearance. It's really in the inner world!

The New You is such a stereotyped concept that we don't want to overstretch the wording. But for lack of a better or more suitable word, and because it's so catchy, let's use it for the remainder of this chapter and book.

So, the New You is a concept for your soul. For your inner being, for your wisdom, for your clarity, for your whole understanding of who you truly are in this bigger concept of life. We'll start with the wisdom that you've been carrying as a soul throughout your travels in the Universe – and yes, most of you have traveled far and carry a lot of wisdom and knowledge from other worlds, but also from earlier times on this planet. This wisdom of who you are and what you are here to do is coded in your DNA – physical and non-physical – and it is coded in your light body as well. It is the trail of breadcrumbs that you've been following throughout all your lifetimes, and also throughout this lifetime. Your higher self is throwing out the breadcrumbs, and your conscious human self is following the trail, just knowing deep inside that this is where you need to go.

Your higher self is really not disconnected from you. It's just the part of you that is directly plugged into the higher realms. Where you have access to infinite wisdom. It's kind of like being connected to the "cloud storage" of the Universe, where you can access *all* of the wisdom with one click of your mouse, and then this wisdom can be channeled or downloaded into the human part of yourself, your human brain and body and DNA, and your human consciousness. But know there is no distinction or disconnect between all of these bodies and parts of you.

So the universal cloud storage contains all of your wisdom and travels and personal information, including the wisdom of what you are meant to do, what you signed up for, what your soul set as your agenda before you came into this present physical incarnation. And your human part doesn't really know what to do unless you were born with your senses open, which is what more and more of the crystal and rainbow children are coming in with. But let's assume that most of the readers are not completely aware of what they are doing here. So the trail of breadcrumbs will inevitably lead you to... *YOU*. To yourself, to your true self, to your revelation of who you truly are. Let's take this concept a step further, and we are now handing back over to the cats. *(The cats come in purring...)*

This is our part where we can show our humans how we *see* their true selves. We can see it, as we are connected to not just our own "cloud" but also to your "cloud". And our soul but also our conscious cat self sees beyond your veil, sees beyond the self that you are trying to portray to the world, that you have trained yourself to show to the outside. We cats *see* your *true* self. The part of you that is infinitely loving, infinitely wise, infinitely powerful.

It's important for us that you know... that we feel, see, perceive the real you. The person or being beyond the fears and limitations and programming. The part of you that you might be afraid to show even yourself or the part you might be afraid to live because you fear persecution, or misunderstanding, or not fitting in. You've been trying so hard to fit in, for people to understand you, for people to like you, that you have forgotten to just be. To just be you. And we cats see, feel, perceive, and know the real you!

Cats help you become the best version of yourself

That is why it's so easy for many people to be around cats, dogs, horses, or other animals. Because you don't have to hide who you are. Because we "get" you. Because we understand you and love you, just the way you are. There is a difference between us cats and other animals, though. What we mean by this is that you are usually portraying a certain tough *YOU* to the dogs (needing to be strict and giving orders, because you are trained to think that dogs need orders), or portraying a certain strict *YOU* to horses (because you think they need commands, because they are so large and you think you need to be tough for them to respect you). You see where this is going, and we know that neither is really true... but we cannot speak for the dogs and horses.

Yet when it comes to cats, people usually don't have any of these preconceived notions of portraying a certain *YOU* to us. They don't try to be tough and give orders or try to be the alpha. With cats, people tend to just be themselves – and many times, their better or best selves! They try to be nice and sweet, so they don't scare us (if you have a timid cat). Or they try to tone down their anger at the world around us (so we don't run away from your angry vibrations). Many people try to please us – and thereby they are living and attuning to the best version of themselves. So this is how we cats actually help you to be the best version of yourself! You want to please us, you want us to stay around you, you want us to cuddle and play with you, to purr for you, and to sit on your lap. To achieve that, you are tuning into the best version of yourself: the mellow part of you, the loving part of you, the relaxed part of you, the wise and knowledgeable part of you.

Let's elaborate on the best version of yourself within the New You concept. This best version is what you bring forth when you are around us cats. None of the bossy version of you. None of the alpha version. None of the "I need to be someone, to show how great I am, to show my best calling card". No, you are just being your gentlest, sweetest, most loving, *and* most playful version of yourself. And yes, this is a part of the cat secret! This is how we cats help you become your best self! This is what sets us apart from dogs and horses and other animals. You do not approach us with the desire of taming us, of milking us, of training us, of subduing us, or any of that other stuff you do with other animals. And we are saying that without judgment. Know that all the animals in your life – or in human society – have their part and their important piece of the puzzle. We are not putting any of that down. Not how you think of them or how your relationship is with them, not what they are providing or doing for you, or the service they are here to contribute to life on Earth.

No, but we cats are here to get out the best in you! The version of you that is truest to yourself in your higher form (the form that is not bound by human thinking or conditioning, and not bound by a physical vessel). So for this reason, it is safe to say that we cats are here for your highest Ascension path, to remind you who you truly are. Free and free-spirited like us. Divine like us. Living in the flow, like us. Playful and joyful like us. Social and friendly like us, with our kind and other kinds. And most of all: you are us in a higher form! We are you in a different form! We all come from the same creation, we are all infused with the same light particles. We share much of your DNA and vice versa. So we are just you in a different manner, but all working towards the same common goal. To provide the best possible life here on this planet for everyone that is on it. And to provide you with the tools you need to further the Ascension process on Earth and beyond.

12

THE ASCENSION TIMELINE

The Ascension is an organic timeline that has been planned for planet Earth since the conception of the modern kind man. The concept has been spun and twisted and used for many different reasons and concepts. Suffice it to say that the Ascension is an organic process, spanning millions of years, and since this planet was originally seeded. It was placed here strategically, as an outpost between your sun and the central sun, which is in the Pleiades cluster. Alcyone is the central sun for this quadrant of the Universe. It has been revealed to many of you that the point of the Ascension is to bring this quadrant of the Universe to a peaceful coexistence with each other, as a "friendly neighborhood" kind of project. So Earth has been a designated peace post for the plan in this quadrant.

Humans have been conceived as the species that would unify all the aspects of Source that had been splintered and caused division. The division – as we explained earlier – was part of the Source project to experience growth. In order for growth to happen, things have to be pushed and expanded and sometimes taken to an extreme. When the extremes started to cause too much conflict, the divine plan started to unfold in the other direction. This meant bringing the extreme factions back together to become unified again – but in a higher, wiser, and more expanded form. So these outposts were created throughout the Universe to bring the factions back into unity. The Ascension plans for Earth were laid millions of years ago, and the seeding was begun when modern humankind was to be brought together from different star nation aspects, to become the modern-day peace project.

Humans are related to different star nations

We have already shared that the human genome was conceived as a unity project, with many different star nations bringing in their specific DNA. Please don't see it as a lab rat project, though, where humans were caged and treated with DNA samples. It was more of an organic evolution of the beings that were already incarnated here on Earth. Their DNA was upgraded over a long period of time, with occasional DNA boosts, but mainly by pairing and organic reproduction with beings that volunteered to incarnate on Earth into a human or human-like body while their DNA slowly mixed with the human DNA, thus upgrading entire lineages with star-infused genome. In this way, it was a very long-term and organic project, not a quick infusion or transplantation of DNA. The beings coming in with star DNA were partially aware of their mission, and they upgraded the human consciousness to the level of where you are now.

At this point, we are ready to address a few of the commonly asked questions, such as: how many star nations placed their DNA into humans? The answer is many, with the obvious ones being the Pleideans, the Sirians, the Arcturians, the Lyrans of course, with much of the Lyran DNA also being in the other star families. This list is not so much about specifics but about the bigger picture. The different star families then became guides for the Earth Ascension process.

So let's say that Angelics put their DNA into humans and the human experience. They then followed up by being there in light form and non-corporeal form, to guide their human brothers and sisters through this project. Many of the beings that are called ascended masters or archangels or other angelic figures have been here in both physical form and ethereal form, and they have been guiding humanity from the get-go. The same goes for Lyrans and the feline species: they have been here for a very long time, as have the Sirians, Pleideans, and others. Some have incorporated to become some of history's greatest figures, such as Jesus and Mary and the Essenes. But also some of the Lyrans have been the greatest figures: Nefereti, for instance, and some other queens or kings of the old. We don't want to go into specifics. The point is that these star brothers and sisters in human form have been steering and guiding humanity into the "right" direction.

Another common question about the Earth project is: why is there so much suffering here? Well, it's because some of the factions were and still are misguided, but that was always part of the long-term plan. In the outposts of Ascension, there was a lot of extreme polarity going on. The vision behind it was that the factions could come together in one place (meaning one planet), and by living together as one multi-faceted species overcome their differences and become one again. That is why humanity is so wooed by many star nations and feared by others. Because you literally carry the best of all the worlds within you, within your beingness, your DNA, and your lifeform. So that you can be the "crown jewel" of this neighborhood project and then spread the acquired peace and the love and the oneness to the entire galaxy.

This was a little excursion into the workings behind the Ascension project and why humanity is so important to this entire project. Let's move on to the specific timeline of Ascension.

The organic Ascension is steadily on track

That being said, know that this is *not* about a certain timing, in the human sense of the word. But it is about the project being moved forward now with a certain fervor, to move Earth and humanity's frequency along with the organic Ascension. The timelines were set a long time ago, but they always shift and change. Not on the biggest of scales, but some of the timelines got distorted. The organic Ascension was actually pushed back a few centuries ago when unknowingness and some of the darker aspects of mankind were brought out by our brothers and sisters from the opposite faction that are – sometimes grudgingly – part of this unity project. So the timelines got distorted a few centuries ago, and the denser aspect of the star nation "guides" had taken over. But not enough for the whole project to be thwarted. It was merely a swing of the pendulum to one of the extremes, which was then counterbalanced by the swing to the other side. The pendulum is now at 80% of the lighter side, just to give you a comparison. The goal or endgame is to reach 100% and then stay and move up into the higher realms for all of Earth and all of humanity. So how do we get to the 100%?

That's where the cats are coming back in. Though not the only ones, but the cats *are* here to guide humans into the higher realms and for the Ascension project to be concluded. The cats are helping to guide "their" humans into the higher frequencies, as well as to awaken the Lyran and feline aspect in humanity to the fruition point.

So in wrapping up this chapter, let's summarize how we shared that the New You is intrinsically connected to the New Earth and the Ascension timeline. As the Ascension project progresses, your New You is coming out to play more and more. As the Ascension frequencies hit Earth and slowly start to integrate and *become* the New Earth, so are you slowly becoming the True You. This is the next step: from the *NEW YOU* (the one who gets lighter and experiences life as easier and with more joy and love) to slowly integrating all these Ascension energies that are upleveling you and every aspect of your frequency and of your life or beingness. Then the Ascension plays out further, and eventually, you'll be the *TRUE YOU*, which is the next chapter we want to share.

13

THE TRUE YOU

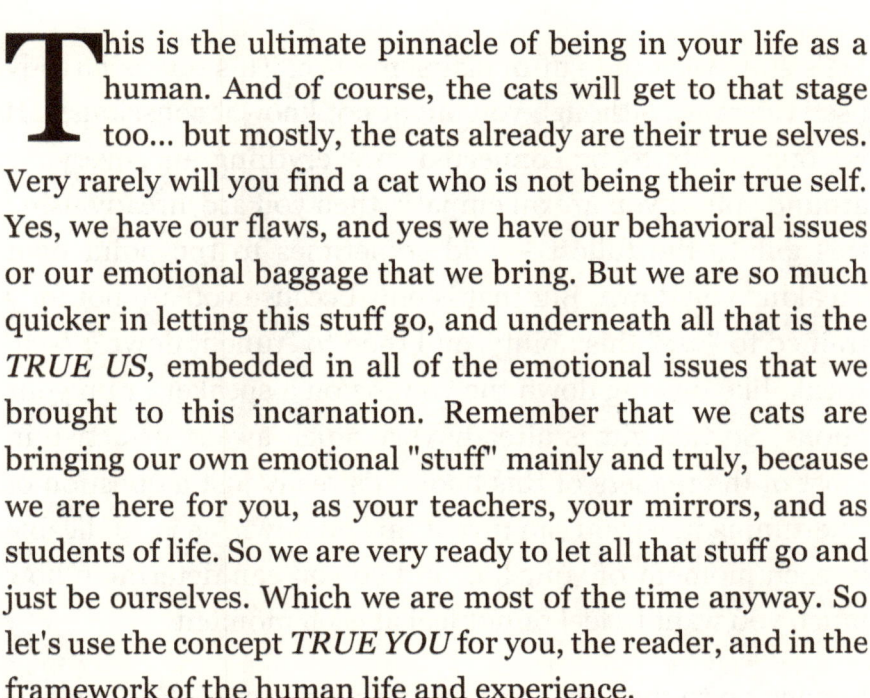

This is the ultimate pinnacle of being in your life as a human. And of course, the cats will get to that stage too... but mostly, the cats already are their true selves. Very rarely will you find a cat who is not being their true self. Yes, we have our flaws, and yes we have our behavioral issues or our emotional baggage that we bring. But we are so much quicker in letting this stuff go, and underneath all that is the *TRUE US*, embedded in all of the emotional issues that we brought to this incarnation. Remember that we cats are bringing our own emotional "stuff" mainly and truly, because we are here for you, as your teachers, your mirrors, and as students of life. So we are very ready to let all that stuff go and just be ourselves. Which we are most of the time anyway. So let's use the concept *TRUE YOU* for you, the reader, and in the framework of the human life and experience.

The True You is a magnificent being, that is not determined by your past. Imagine a way of living, where you are truly connected to all that you are: that means your natural gifts of claircognizance, clairvoyance, clairaudience, and of course clairsentience. All of you have these gifts or abilities embedded in your consciousness and soul plan. Some of you are already using them, or some of them, to a certain level. But all of it is so ready to come out for you to use it, for you to revel in it, and for you to experience life on this plane to the fullest!

Exploring your clairsenses

Let's start with the gift of clairsentience. This one is already used the most, although you might not know it consciously. It is your ability to be connected to everything and everyone around you. If you are an empath, then you are already using this gift to the fullest – and sometimes to the point of it breaking you down. But that is only because you are not fully trained to "use" this ability, and then to "tune it down", so to speak, like turning down the volume on a speaker or on your phone. So this gift is already very much awake or active in most of the readers of this book. It's really just a question of fine-tuning it, so you can turn it up and down, as is applicable in each moment of your life, and so you can determine how much you want to feel or not feel at each moment.

Moving on to the next ability: your clairvoyance. Yes, most of you already have this channel open, whether you know it or not. Every time you go into meditation, you are most likely tapping into this ability. You use it when you visualize something or when you see something with your inner eye. The more you use and tone this ability, the more it will come online. For those who are not yet using this, suffice it to say that there might have been an instant in childhood or prior life where you were ridiculed for what you "saw" or you were told that it isn't right to "see" things that weren't physically there. Yes, we are talking about seeing beyond the veil, and seeing fairies or light beings in your room or in the forest, when you were a child. It was not your imagination or an isolated incident that you were seeing this! For your ability of clairvoyance lies not only in your imagination or ability of visualization. No, it's also the ability to see into other dimensions (which cats possess as well, even more so than humans), and it is the ability to also see into the future. This is the most commonly meant ability when humans speak of clairvoyance, but it's not really the correct use of the term. Yes, you can also travel into a future scenario, but that requires combining several of your abilities to do so.

But this ability to "see beyond" is alive and active in most of you, whether you know it or not. And it is a beautiful ability to have, because it helps you and serves you in creation – in creating the life that you want, the circumstances that you want, and tapping into other realms and other possibilities out there. So for most of the readers, this ability is already active. If you have trouble accessing your "inner seeing", then there are exercises to sharpen this tool, and you can look up how to clear and cleanse your pineal gland – the organ through which inner seeing is facilitated. But really, most of all, trust your instincts on this one! Don't be afraid of *seeing* things, as everything you see and perceive is actually helping your journey and strengthening your clairsenses muscles.

Communicating with the higher realms

Let's go to the next ability: your clairaudience. This is a big one for most people! Many Ascension seekers and truth seekers and awakening souls want to *hear* their higher guidance more clearly. So they practice and practice to call in their spirit guides or other beings in the higher realms that they communicate with, but then are disappointed if they don't *hear* their messages. At this point, let us assure you: there is nothing wrong with your inner hearing nor with your ability to communicate with these higher realms. It is usually just a misunderstanding that you expect to hear voices that speak into your inner ear.

The truth is that most humans don't really hear voices when they communicate with the higher realms. It is more of a channeling of words, thoughts, concepts, images, and a *knowing* that gets communicated in different ways. Look at it as packets of information that get downloaded into your system, to use an example of modern-day technology. Imagine that you are asking a question in, say, a chat communication tool. You ask a one-liner question, and the person on the other side of the chatroom answers this in a comprehensive manner and sends you back a 1,000-word description as the answer. Imagine this answer (or the 1,000 words) coming back at the click of a button on that end. You will receive this long 1,000-word answer all at one time. As your eyes read through all the lines that come back to you, your brain is putting together the answer, so you can understand what was said. So the question was simple, and the answer was comprehensive, and it'll take your brain a while to put together and compute the long answer, despite it having been downloaded into your computer in one split second.

Now apply that same example to a conversation with the higher realms. You in your human mode formulate a question with your mind and send it into the ether. The beings in the higher realms will formulate an answer, and let's say this is a comprehensive 1,000-word answer. They will press the "send" button and literally download it into your consciousness. You'll get this really comprehensive answer all in one split second... and then your brain will start to decipher and bring it into your human mind to conceive and understand.

So for some of you, the answer might actually come as a voice into their inner hearing... and you'll hear the sentences in the order that you can understand it, in a linear fashion. For others, and this is more common, it's more like a sequence of thoughts, like the download we described above. And they wonder: *Are these my own thoughts, or am I just imagining it, or is this really the Divine or the higher beings speaking to me through my thoughts?* In most cases, it'll be the latter, and yes, you are getting the long packet answer in the form of linear thoughts forming in your mind. For others, it'll be more like a channeling, as in, the words coming out of your mouth, without you really knowing where they come from.

And yet for others, they'll just have this packet of information in their consciousness and they'll just know – without words – what was being said. They just *know* the answer, without having consciously *thought* about it. And yet for others – and this is the last form of understanding the higher realms – they'll see images or pictures or a scene of the information that is being shared (the 1,000-word explanation) and they'll then decipher or explain the pictures. In any case, you just communicated with the Divine or the higher realms, be it your spirit guides or star family or any entity in other dimensions. And you received your answer, without having *heard* it as a voice in your head. The point we are making is that it really doesn't matter *how* you get your answers. Just be happy and excited that your clairsenses are working, and that you are communicating with the higher realms!

We'd like to mention here that we cats are always communicating with the higher realms, the higher consciousness, and also with you, our dear humans. Yes, this is the cats coming in now, and they are wanting to explain that you can also talk to us, your beloved cats (or dogs or horses or any other animal) in the same manner. Just formulate your question (in the form of words, spoken out loud or quietly in your mind), and then be open to receive whatever answer comes in. You might be surprised to hear, feel, see, or just *know* the answer that was coming back from us. But that is for another book to explore further.

Being connected to cosmic consciousness

Let's move on to the last of the clairsenses we wanted to talk about: your claircognizance. This one is quite sublime, as it is the culmination of all of the above. In this state, and with this ability honed or wide open, you'll be able to tap into any realm, any being, any concept, and any time-space continuum that you want to communicate with. All of the above play a part in being truly claircognizant. When all your communication channels are wide open, then you'll truly have tapped into your potential of being a conduit of pure light, of the Divine, and of all of creation.

At this point, we the cats, want to share for a moment that we are always in our full capability of claircognizance, clairaudience, clairvoyance, and clairsentience. When we are experiencing our world, all of these channels are always open. That is why you perceive us as being connected to the Universe, as we are channeling this book for you, and connected to an infinite pond of wisdom that is out there. We are freely tapping into this ocean of wisdom or cosmic collective consciousness. That is why we are able to give you advice on how to see or do things, or how to manage your process of Ascension or even insights into your soul's journey and life path. When we see you struggling or not knowing what to do in a certain situation, we merely "plug in" to this ocean of wisdom and cosmic consciousness. Then, we "download" the answer for you or what your soul needs to hear. It's actually less of a plugging in, as we are naturally connected to this sea of consciousness. So are you, dear human, but you are not always aware of it.

This explains why we cats know so well what to tell you about how to shape your journey of truth, wisdom seeking, and fulfilling your soul contracts and your soul's journey. We are merely the vessels through which the wisdom flows, so we can guide you on your path and help you gain access to this ocean of wisdom yourself. This also explains why we, the cats, volunteered to write or channel this book to the author, as the ocean of wisdom runs through us, as the words are flowing out of her writing hands. That is why the higher beings or divine wisdom comes through us, the cats, as we are channelers just as much as the author is.

So yes, the cats are very much able to use all the above abilities and are naturally "connected" to universal consciousness. And we are here to help and facilitate you, the reader, to learn to be connected to all these abilities and gifts that you are born with.

Thus, the True You – going back to that concept – is being in a state in which you effortlessly reach into these abilities and use them in your daily life, to create the life you have always dreamed of or, in most cases, even better.

The True You is someone who is deeply connected to your cosmic roots. Who is highly aware of everyone and everything around you, and your connection to the whole – as in the human experience and the Ascension project you signed up for, and as in your divine mission in this lifetime.

And lastly, the True You is someone who has the ability to love fully: to love life, to love yourself in your human form, to love your surroundings, to love the other humans, to love the project you serve on, and to love life itself.

Let's conclude this chapter by saying that the True You is the state you're going into. So don't be upset that you are not in that state yet. Yes, there are other abilities and facets to that state. The opening of your clairsenses and your state of love and joy constitutes being the True You: fully open and aware and connected to who you are, what you can do, and what you are here to do while serving in the bigger picture. And then living in love and joy and purposeful creation.

14

YOUR SPARK OF CREATION

We would like to guide you through a process of discovering your true self and tapping into your spark of creation. Just for a moment, we invite you to close your eyes and put your feet firmly on the ground. Then, surround yourself with love – true, unfiltered, and unconditional love. You can do this any way that you can feel this love. If you have a hard time just feeling love, then think of your cat. Feel the love that your cat is giving you. Or the love you feel when you look at your cat. Or any of your loved ones. Wherever you feel the most love, this is the object or being that you can focus on. Now feel this love like a nebula, like a cloud of pink or golden or white light around you. Feel it building up into a thick, fluffy cloud around you. Like a cloud you want to fall back into and enjoy its fluffiness.

Now imagine yourself floating in this fluffy cloud. You are lying comfortably on your back, and this cloud is taking you higher and higher, into the sky and out into the Universe. All you have to do is lay still in all this fluffy goodness and just enjoy the ride. We are taking you higher and higher and to the edge of the known Universe. Now look down and marvel at all this wonder underneath you... all the planets and stars, and all the life you feel teeming in there. Humans, humanoids, animals, plants, minerals, crystals, etc. Feel as much of this wonder as possible. Now look up into what you thought was dark nothingness. Now you see it really is like a star-speckled sky above you. These stars you see are all like diamonds, they are sparkling and inviting. And now realize how you are one of these stars! You are one sparkle in a sea of consciousness. This sea is inviting you to join now. Delve into this sea of consciousness, this ocean of sparkles.

You'll feel like you are surrounded by fellow stars, fellow sparkles. See and feel how you are part of this wonderful one-ness, like an ocean. But you are still your *YOU* particle. Feel how this *YOU* particle is now splitting away from the ocean. You still feel and realize you are a part of this wonderful ocean of sparkles, of lights. But you are also a *YOU* particle, which is now splitting and going off on its own course. You are taking the sparkleness and the knowledge and the wholeness of this wonderful thing, this source cloud of consciousness, with you on your journey. And yet, you are on your own, exploring the wonderful vast cosmos and Universe underneath you.

So feel or see yourself floating back down on your fluffy cloud, which is now more a sparkling golden cloud... and you are floating back down through the Universe, until you see planet Earth in all her blue glory, underneath you. See or feel yourself float towards her, now with a distinct recognition or knowledge of how you are here as a representative, as a spark of this sparkling unity consciousness. But you are also here as *YOU*, as your wonderful sparkle that came here with the distinct mission of being *YOU*, of bringing this wonderful sparkling ocean of consciousness here to this planet. Of shaping this planet in the way you want to contribute, so all beings on this planet can become one again and bring the sparkling and loving Source consciousness ocean onto this planet.

As you are descending, your mission becomes clearer and clearer, for on the way, you also make experiences, and you might just now understand how important your contribution here to this planet is. You understand how you are here to make it sparkle and shine, like that whole other world up there where you come from – where we all come from.

So this is how you understand or experience your unique beingness. Your consciousness comes from Source and once split off as a wonderful spark. While being connected to Source and to the whole that created this Universe, you are still *YOU* with your own distinct way of being, of feeling, and of creating. And this here right now, your current lifetime, is your time to shine, to create, to be, and to bring *all* of your sparkles to this planet that you call home at this point in time.

Realize you are a sparkle in the sea of consciousness

Now the cats are taking over. This sparkle of consciousness that is *YOU* is the reason you are here. It is the reason why you breathe, feel, live, love, it is the reason why you *are* in this beautiful body, in this beautiful lifetime, on this beautiful planet. Just like you humans are a sparkle of consciousness of the whole sea of creation, so are we cats! We all come from this same place, and some chose to be a human or humanoid sparkle, and some chose to be in a different form. It does not mean one is better than the other. We are just all different forms and ideas of creation.

You can see where we are going with this. First, we wanted to give you a taste or an understanding of what Source consciousness feels like and where you, your consciousness is truly from. In this next step, we'll guide you into the process of understanding your task, your willingly taken tasks, and your purpose, that you chose to incarnate here on Earth with.

We cats are truly here to help you find and follow your purpose, or facilitate your path. We and you both are here with a distinct purpose and mission, to help further this planet's evolution and – remember – to connect the field of consciousness on this beautiful blue planet Earth, to bring it into contact and direct connection with the ocean of golden sparkles of Source consciousness.

Of course, Mother Earth is connected as well. But the consciousness level on this planet is somewhat subdued and not of the highest golden Source vibration – yet. All our combined tasks here are to bring the collective field of this planet in direct alignment of vibration with Source consciousness. That is what we are all here to accomplish: to bring all of creation onto the vibration of its Source, which is pure consciousness – a sea of love.

As a result, this planet is exemplary. We are all here to witness the miracle of a new planet, a new consciousness to be born. And all of us – humans and animals and plants alike – are here to help facilitate this birth, this wonder of creation of a new life form. The planet with all its inhabitants will go into the next level of vibration, of consciousness. We are all here to play our part. We have already explained the cats' mission and the cats' tasks in this process: to help humans align to your highest task and vibration. And to elevate the vibration of the planet as a whole, by our innate beingness in the love and joy frequencies.

The human soul essence groups

Let's now take a moment to look at the typical tasks of humans in this process. It won't take as long as our cats' tasks, but it has everything to do with aligning you with your highest purpose and frequency. Let's start by saying that the humans' tasks are more diverse than ours, but they are inherently the same. To bring your uniqueness to this experience, to this project Earth here, but still to unify at a common cause, which is to bring the higher frequencies into this planet's experience. For us cats, it is the love and joy and freedom frequencies. For you humans, it's similar but more: you are to bring the sparkle of creation itself here! Yes, you are here to create the highest outcome possible. By doing this for yourself and your own life here, you elevate the whole.

So really, this is the *true* secret of this book: you humans are here to elevate yourself to the highest creation frequency you can muster in this human body. To realize that you are an integral part of creation itself. So be yourself, express yourself in any way, shape, or form that wants to come through you. This is how you elevate the frequency of creation on this planet.

15

THE 12 HUMAN ARCHETYPES OF CREATION

In this chapter, we'll be sharing the human soul essence archetypes of your purpose here on Earth, and how you contribute to the creation process of the whole.

We encourage you to *feel* into which categories you fall, as you are digging deeper to understand your purpose in the creative experience. It's not so much about figuring it out with your conscious mind, but more so to have a deep *knowing* which category is yours. It will resonate very deeply with you, and there won't be much soul searching necessary to find your purpose, your category, your place in this puzzle. Note that you might fall into two or even three categories, but there is usually one predominant one, just like with the cats. And in order to keep up with the cats, we'll start with an easy one.

✸ THE LOVER

Some humans are part of the "love frequency" group. Like us lover cats, their part is to bring and anchor the highest love frequencies possible into this planetary experience. This is how they create! They create a sea, a network of love on this planet, by loving their family, their community, their co-workers, or by spreading their network of love around the world through online platforms, social media, and other online communities.

The lovers are much the same as their cat counterparts, so we won't go into much more detail. Suffice it to say that these lover archetypes not only spread love, but also teach love, and help others that have shut their hearts off, to feel love again. For more details of the lover archetype, look at the respective cat chapter earlier in the book. We are closely related, after all.

✸ THE ARTIST

The next group of humans anchoring in the highest creative frequencies are the artists. We mean artists of any way, shape, or form, and we are talking about true, organic art, like the painters and the musicians of this world. Or the people who contribute wonderful pottery and plant art in gardening. Or those who create beautiful clothes, drapery, or anything to do with using shapes, colors, and materials to its highest pleasing and creative form. Yes, we even include architects here who are designing homes, structures, streets, houses, buildings, and all other creations. Cars, even! All of this creative artistry is a form of love for creation, be it that the art is expressed on a canvas, or in a digital piece of music, or in the form of a beautiful and striking building that goes up on your street. All of this creative, artistic expression contributes to a wonderful way of living on this planet.

✸ THE HEALER

The third group is quite interesting and diverse: these are the healers, the doctors, the nurses, and the health practitioners of any kind. Also the entire medical system in its truest form which originated from a calling to help and heal people. To help them get better, to overcome their bodily limits, and to heal their physical ailments. Any type of energy healer or alternative practitioner who works to balance the body, mind, and soul of people belongs in this category. So does anything related to healing at all – be it emotional healing, or spiritual healing, or mental healing, and of course, physical healing. We would even include dieticians or physical exercise professionals in this group, such as people who work as trainers for the physical wellbeing of others, in gyms or other facilities. For this is all in the name of healing and nourishing and keeping the physical body at its best and highest functioning level.

✸ THE SCHOLAR

The next group of purposes for humans are typically the writers and teachers and scholars. The ones who bring knowledge and wisdom into this world and the human experience. In the cat comparison, these are the teachers who are here to help you learn things. This human category, the scholars, are here to anchor in ancient teachings and to educate the masses. As you have all come here born with a veil, not remembering your past lifetimes, there is so much to read, learn, research, and experience, and much to pass on to those humans who are not studying the ancient mysteries, the old teachings, and the records of what came before. So the scholars are quite interesting and very important to have here. We include the teachers and researchers and even most of the scientists in here. Although, as a note, scientists can also fall into the artist and other categories. But let's move on.

✸ THE LIGHTBRINGER

The next one is the wonderful art of being you! Yes, we said it. For this category, it's all about being the shining light that you are. These precious humans are here to just be themselves, to lead by example, and to create everything from a state of deep knowing, of being who they are, and of teaching, creating, healing by just being themselves. The closest in the cat categories would be the muse. So when you are in this category, then you just *know*. You might have resonated with the healer, the teacher, the creative artist... but now you know that you have a bit of all of it. And your greatest driving force in life might be to know that you just *have* to teach, but you don't do it the conventional way... instead, you find you have a natural knack for teaching those who ask you for help. Or you might feel you are a healer, but you do so naturally, without having to make a big fuss about it. Or you like to sing, paint, draw, or make clothes, but you are not driven by having to put your work out there and share it with *everyone* in the world. You'll just do your artwork and share it with whoever comes across it. So if this is you, then know that your ultimate task here is to just *BE*... and just be *YOU*! You will lead by example, you will shine your light naturally, and you will elevate everyone's vibration around you by just being you.

✳ THE PRIEST/ESS

This next category is an important one and different from the cats: the priest, or priestess. These are truly the divine messengers. They are the ones who not only aggregate and pass on the teachings but come up with them! They are the ones not just doing the healings, but anointing others to do them! Yes, this is almost a sacred task, and not every healer or teacher falls into this category. If you feel within now – and you felt touched by being a healer or a scholar, but you feel what you are doing goes beyond that – then you are a priest/ess. Know that you came here with a high decree of leading, of sharing knowledge, of leading others into this new world. If you feel touched by this, then you are likely a priest/ess.

You are here by divine decree. You've been here for a *very* long time. You came here with the knowledge of the elders and were most likely here for the ancient cultures of Lemuria, Atlantis, Egypt, and beyond. You came here with the will to create this beautiful experience. You've been leading and heralding in every new age. You've been here also as a leader of teams and as a liaison with the ancient cultures and the elders on other planets that have been overseeing this project Earth for millennia. In short, if you are a priest/ess, then you'll know that you have a sacred task and mission, and you'll put your message out into the world to lead by divine decree.

✱ THE VISIONARY

The next one is the visionary, or the leader, the one that is at the forefront of new movements. This might be on the level of technology. Or on the level of politics and leading whole countries. Or on the level of thought movement. Yes, the thought leaders are in this group, just like the presidents of countries or big corporations. So the leader is obviously here to lead, and we are not spending much time in this category, as it is so obvious. Suffice it to say that *all* leaders are here to further their cause, whether you might perceive their creations and their effects as good or bad. All of it is part of the universal creation and of the integration process on planet Earth, which is to bring *all* facets of this creation back into balance, or back into the whole.

✱ THE AMBASSADOR

The next one is quite magical and mysterious and obvious at the same time. It's the ambassador – for everything, but mainly for creations on or off planet. You are here as an ambassador for the star beings, for your lineage, for your star nation. If this resonates with you, then you'll know that you are here on behalf of the Lyrans, the Sirians, the Pleidians, or others. The star representatives have incarnated here on Earth to bring in the ancient wisdom from other star systems and other planets. They help humans evolve, so they can become a cosmic nation themselves. The ambassadors are here to help bridge the differences and to foster the understanding that it is time for humanity to meet their galactic brothers and sisters.

The starseed cats are the closest to this category. If you feel this is you, then this is your mission and purpose: to bridge the gap between the species, to bring in the galactic frequencies, and to help herald in a new age where humanity will be able to connect to their galactic heritage and to meet their star families.

At this point, we want to address a question: does this mean that all starseed souls are ambassadors? We'll say no, only the ones with that driving spark and mission to bridge the species, to channel messages, and to communicate teachings or galactic knowledge. Other starseeds are here as healers, or gridworkers, or leaders, or priests, or other categories. So no, not all starseeds are ambassadors, but some are.

✳ THE JOYBRINGER

The next type of human tasks is very simple: comparative to our feline joybringer, they are the ones that keep people happy. These are the entertainers, comedians, actors, and also the ones that help with human beauty, design, fashion, etc.

We'd like to call them the human joybringers for now. These are the types that help evolve people's joy frequencies by focusing on fun and playfulness, but also for pleasing and stimulating people's sense of love, joy, ease, and beauty. Surrounding yourself with the good things in life is a feat that is very important to humans. The humor and the laughing part are important, but also the part of beauty and playfulness, and enjoying life with all your senses.

Embracing all the beautiful stuff in life is as important as laughing. Why? Because it makes you feel good. And when you feel good, then you are in the joyful frequencies. Humans – unlike cats – are very strongly connected to their sense of seeing and anything visual, hence anything that *looks* good and pleases your visual senses will bring you joy. It's as simple as that! What for cats is our sense of smell, is for humans your sense of vision. So anything that pleases your eyes, will fall into this category and bring you joy. And anything joyful is very important on your journey to becoming your best self because feeling good means you are vibrating on a higher level. And, ultimately, vibration is what brings you more and more into the realms of the Ascension process.

✳ THE EARTH HEALER

Let's continue the list by adding a very important member of humanity: the Earth healers, also called the healers of the grid or the Earth workers. Some of them are humans, meaning what you call Earth seeds, and some are from far away, what you call starseeds. But they are working closely together in healing the Earth, the grids, the land, the oceans, the seas, the crystalline kingdom, the leylines, and so on. Their work is very important for the whole, for if there is no Earth, there cannot be the experience which everyone here signed up for. So the Earth workers are some of the basic building blocks for the experience. It doesn't mean that the others aren't as important, but the Earth workers do the healing of the main protagonist of this experience: Mother Gaia Sophia, or Earth, or the New Earth. Suffice it to say that there is much more to this Earth worker, but we'll leave it at that. If you are a gridworker, Earth worker, or healer of the crystalline kingdom, then you'll have an inherent knowledge and understanding of what you are here for, and you don't need any explanation or cheering on. You just know what you have to do.

If you are not sure: this is also partially the category for those who work with vortices, stargates, as well as ancient and sacred sites around the planet. But some of those people are also in the priest/ess category. You'll usually instinctively know which type you are when you are in this line of work. Some work with the land or the location itself (likely an Earth healer) and some with the ancient knowledge of rituals and structures that were placed on these lands. In the latter case, you're a priest/ess that is invoking the old rituals and magical connections that are to be made at that site.

✸ THE LIGHT WARRIOR

Let's move on to the next one, and yes, there is a warrior caste in the mix that we like to call light warriors. They are directly needed in this experience, for if there were no protectors or guardians of the human race (and the animals, plants, land masses, oceans, etc.), then this experience would have been short-lived. So they are indeed needed: the ones that defend the species and the lands (not in the form of countries, but in the form of protecting the trees, and the streams, and the minerals, etc. from any harm done). The light warriors are here to protect from outside intruders, but also to protect from within. Whenever there are distortions coming up, the light warriors step in. They defend their brothers and sisters, but also the animals and the vegetation. So anyone you call an activist in your day and age will fall into this category. It doesn't matter if his cause is the ocean, the air, the animals, or any particular group of people, just know that the activists have a sacred duty to protect and to maintain. This is what they are here to do, and they do deserve our deepest gratitude for keeping us all safe.

✸ THE DIVINE MOTHER

The last archetype we want to mention here are the kings and queens, but not in the sense of how you understand them. They are the ones that take on the hardest of all jobs and possibilities: giving life. Yes, we are talking about motherhood and being the divine mother. There are many starseeds that are giving birth to new starseed souls coming into this life right now. These newborn children are the ones that come unburdened from past lifetimes. They are the ones that come either straight from Source, as a completely new spark of consciousness, or they come from the realm of the Divine, as little angels or what you call the rainbow or crystal children. They are pure and unscathed, and they are the ones who, with their vibration, will shift the planetary grids in a much smoother and faster manner, and they will have so much love and joy doing it. They do it on autopilot, without even knowing it.

This category includes the divine motherhood of women who are bringing these children onto the planet, but also the ones that bore children that have brought about great changes to this planet and beyond. Mother Mary is one in this archetype, but there are many other mothers out there who are contributing to this field, and who bring the highest of vibrations into this experience just by being divine mothers and anchoring in lots of love, light, and joy.

There is also the divine fatherhood archetype, but it is more rare and not that pronounced at this time in history. They have been shaping the human experience for the last couple tens of thousands of years, with their patriarchal way of doing things. They are, however, handing much of their clout now to the divine mothers, which is why we are not specifically including them in the 12 human archetypes.

Where to go from here

This chapter illuminated much of why you are here, what your special archetype is, and what you, the reader, are contributing to this Earth experience. If you did not find yourself in these categories, don't feel overwhelmed or upset. There are many more examples of where you fit into this picture, and there are always special souls on a special mission. But that being said, you should just go with your intuition or gut, and whatever category resonates most with you, that's who you are in this grand tapestry of human creation.

By presenting these 12 human archetypes of purpose and creation, we wanted to give you a chance to come home to yourself, so to speak. To find yourself welcomed by your soul essence group, or your archetype group, so you know what your highest expression is, and what you contribute to this planet and the Ascension process.

Know that whether you are a healer or a scholar or a light warrior, there is always room for expansion. It doesn't mean that this is what your soul's one fixed archetype is, but what expression you are currently bringing to this universal experience. As with everything, people are different in their soul expression, with some being very specific, and others very expansive in their soul's journey throughout the ages.

There are souls that are very much tuned into one thing that they do. Let's take as an example someone who is an ambassador. It's the core of what their entire soul spark experience is about, and they feel a very strong connection to being the eternal ambassador for a certain group (let's say for everything feline in the Universe). This ambassador will then spend lifetime after lifetime being a spokesperson for the feline races, and bring this specific mission into different worlds.

And then there are others that are the opposite: not an expression of one mission or one star family, but they are a kaleidoscope of things. They carry many star family expressions in them, and their mission might be to be very expansive and to bring together all the species in a myriad of ways. These might be healers or priest/esses, or both combined, and they work their magic touching many people and factions at the same time. And they have done so for millennia and will do so for many more.

And then there are yet other souls that chose to have very different experiences during their journey throughout the ages. They were, say, light warriors in other realms, such as the Lyran or Orion conflicts, but then chose to come to Earth and become gridworkers, to switch things up and experience a whole different way of being than before. Much like actors in the human realm: some choose a career where they are being typecast in always the same kind of roles, and they thrive and enjoy every bit of it. And then there are other actors who like to explore different genres and play very different roles. They are the bad guy in some roles, and then the shiniest good guy hero in others. And they love the diversity and wouldn't want to have it any other way.

The same goes for the human experience and the soul's experience in this universal game. You choose if you want to be the same expression over a long period of time, or if you want to explore all the facets out there for your personal experience.

What's coming next? The human experience and how *YOU* can evolve, so you can bring your highest joy, expression, and love to the table.

16

HOW CATS SHIFT YOUR ENERGY

This chapter is all about you and how to shift your energy and your beingness to become the New You and eventually the True You. We are wrapping up your journey with the tools you need to go forward and to move into the higher frequencies.

There are many things you can do to shift your energy: to move, to sing, to love, to experience with all your senses (like the cats do), etc. But there is one predominant thing you can do, and we mean in your daily life, that will infuse more love and joy frequencies into your life: spending time with your cat.

Yes, we said it! And now we are bringing the story arch back to your beloved felines. For they are the reason you picked up this book, and they are the reason why you've been reading and learning about all of this. As the cats are co-creating this book, we want you to know that they are very much aware of all of this wisdom. Remember how they are dipped into the sea of knowledge and just *know* these things!

We know you picked up this book because you wanted to learn about your cat, and then we took you on a detour to learn about yourself. Now, we are bringing this full circle back to your cat. So you as a cat lover have a *huge* advantage over other people. You have the best energy worker in terms of love and joy frequencies right there next to you, in your own home.

The cats are taking over now, coming back in. We, the cats, are here very much for your frequency exchange with the Universe. We are here to help you bridge the gaps of your human frequency, which is much in the lower spectrum, with all the fear and anger going on for large parts of humanity. But you also have the higher frequencies available, which are just waiting for you to dip your toes in! And not just dipping, we want you to fully dive in, to immerse yourself into these frequencies as much and as fully as you can!

So how do you do that, you probably want to know. Easy: ask your cat! Yes, your cat will know what *YOU* specifically need, in order for you to reach the higher vibrations of love and joy. She will accompany you and show you the way.

How the cat archetypes support you

In the following section, we'll go back to the archetypes and tell you how each representative of our species can help you reach the higher frequencies. Let's go through them, as a handbook reference.

♥ THE LOVER

He will guide you with his love. He will teach you love. He will immerse you with his loving vibes until you are so drenched in the love frequencies that you'll stay there more permanently. We are not talking about this happening overnight. But just know and be aware that when you have a lover cat, then your task is to bathe in his frequencies, to learn from him, and to just follow his lead. Try to match his frequencies or moods, until you reach that same or a similar state. Remember the tuning fork, and let your cat and his energy guide the way.

♥ THE JOYBRINGER

Same as above. He is an easy one to follow, and we might even add, he is easier. By just being himself, he will shower you with joy energies as much as you need them. He will do his funny antics, or he will just be so cute or so lovely that your heart goes out and you cannot *not* smile! So how do you harness the most out of this companion? Spend time with him. Let his irresistible manner be your guiding force, and your go-to anchor whenever you feel down. Eventually, he will pull you into the higher frequencies, whether you notice it or not. Just let it happen, let him do his magic, and follow his lead. He'll bring joy, fun, and love into your life – lots of it, for you!

♥ THE SUPPORTER

This one will also take you by his hand – or paw – and just lead the way. Let him be there for you, lean on him when you need it, but also be grateful for his energetic and physical support during your journey in the more material realms. Of course, he will also be there to support you emotionally and in a higher sense, but he will mainly be your guiding light, like a star, guiding you through the corridors of everyday life. Let him shine his light and be your support, and you'll be attuning to his gentle, kind, and strong energies. He'll automatically shift you to the higher frequencies of feeling love and joy over the fact that he is with you every step of the way.

♥ THE SOULMATE

Oh, the precious soulmate. He will be your everything on the way! Much of what we said about the three previous cats will conglomerate here in this one. The soulmate will not only be your guide into the love frequencies (because you love him *so much*), but also your joybringer (because you cherish his company *so much*), and of course your supporter (because he helps you *so much*). So the soulmate can supercharge your experience if you let him work his magic on all these levels. You can get there so much faster with a soulmate cat by your side. Getting into the love and joy frequencies for longer periods at a time is at your fingertips right here, right now. All you have to do is let your soulmate cat purr the way.

♥ THE HEALER

This one has a built-in fail safe mechanism. The reason why we think she has almost magical capabilities is that she can do it all for you! When you have a healer cat, then you can ask her to magically bring you into these desired frequency states. Your healer cat will do everything in her power to heal your denser aspects, so you can transmute your "stuff" and truly align yourself with the love and joy frequencies. Note that if you are a healer yourself or do healing work, then you might be taking on some of your clients' emotional charge. But it doesn't have to be that way. You can protect yourself and still do healing work. Just find your own way to not take on what you do for others. And ask your healer cat (and you most likely have one by your side), to protect you and to heal *you,* as you are going through your journey. So the love and joy frequencies, in this case, can be brought to you by your healer cat. Just ask!

♥ THE ENERGY WORKER

This archetype supports you in much of the same ways as the healer cat – the difference being that he will be actively working with your field. He will shift the field and the energy around you, in your home, in your bodies, in your aura, in your family, in your relationships, so that *you* have space to grow and come into your own energy. The main distinction is that while the healer cat will use healing energies to shift *your* energy, the energy worker will shift your outside world and the energy *around* you. But the principle is the same. So just ask your energy worker cat to help you shift into the love and joy frequencies, and he will go about it and help you achieve what you need.

By the way, know that the cats are naturally already doing all of what we are describing here. As they are dipped into the sea of consciousness and universal wisdom, they inherently know their archetypes and respective tasks. But through your awareness of it, you can now actively participate and ask them to tweak it here and there. And, more importantly, you can be fully aware of the benefits your cat is giving you, so that you can actively *receive*.

So really, your – the human's – part in this is simple: to receive the gifts your cat bestows on you. The gift of being close to you, and attuning you to the higher frequencies. But let's continue with the archetypes.

♥ THE MIRROR

This cat, as we know, is quite marvelous, and she has her special ways of getting you into the higher frequencies. By pushing you into the right direction, or by holding the mirror in front of you so that you may recognize your own patterns and behaviors, you'll automatically uplevel into the higher frequencies. That is, if or when you are ready to embrace the task, the challenge, the journey, the message, and the wisdom that comes through. Once you realize what needs to be done, you are automatically on a path to completing the task. It's as simple as that. Just knowing the issue or challenge will actually bring you closer to its resolution. This is meant to be a consolation to those who think they are aware of their old patterns but seem to not be able to overcome them.

Know that the path is part of the resolution, and the more the pattern gets brought up, the more it gets unraveled. Observe how every time your issue pops back into your focus, you do a little more dissolving, and a little more unraveling – like a salt rock that gets dissolved a little more each time the water wave hits it. Can it be unnerving that it keeps popping back up? Yes, maybe. But also know that the solution lies in the path of dissolving it. So the mirror cat will eventually push you into the higher frequencies by helping you dissolve your patterns a little more each time. And the more you are shifting into the higher vibrations, your mirror cat will be right alongside you, and then you can *both* enjoy the love and joy frequencies. They'll get stronger and more durable the more you reach them and the more you allow yourself to bathe and revel in them. It's like training a muscle: the more you do it, the longer lasting the effects.

♥ THE MUSE

This one is *always* in the love and joy frequencies. Why? Because it's her very nature! As much as the joybringer lives in his innate joy frequencies, and the lover being in the innate love frequencies, the muse is reveling in both. She will automatically attune you to her frequencies every time you are around her. Therefore, not much needs to be said about this wonderful specimen, except to go with it! Allow yourself the luxury to revel in the love and joy frequencies, for as long as you want to. Because that is what you are here to do. To enjoy life, and yes, to create as well, but to have joy and fun on the way.

A little note about fun and joy: you might be wondering if fun or living in joy isn't done at the expense of others. Many lightworkers bring up this question, and there is a simple answer. The more you are in the higher frequencies of love and joy, the less it will be at the expense of others. We are not talking about fun as in "take a cheap shot at someone and then revel in their misfortune". We are talking about being joyful with your creations. Being purposeful with your creations. Getting yourself, your loved ones, your community, your co-workers, and everyone around you into a joyful mood, and making the world a better place with your creations. There is no falseness here. When you create with an open, loving heart, then your creations cannot hurt anyone.

But beware of thinking that your joy can cause someone else heartache. For when you are truly living a great, joyful life, reveling in your creations which have a positive impact on the world, then you will inspire others to do the same. We are not saying don't have empathy or sympathy for others. We are not saying don't help others out. But it needs to be done with an open heart and a true desire to perform this service. If your service (to help out) is done with a heavy heart or even with dishonesty or inner dissatisfaction (when you do something because you think you have to do it, but it really causes you pain or stress), then you are not always doing a good service, especially when you do this over a long period of time. You will not have a lasting effect on those you help when you do it grudgingly. Therefore, try to have a happy heart when you do or perform a service. And when it doesn't make you happy over a long period of time, then shift your focus to helping someone out in a way that does give you satisfaction and joy in the long run.

Now let's return to the cat archetypes and how you can harness their powers to help shift your energy.

♥ THE TEACHER

This one is a splendid specimen, and she can – of course – teach you to be in the higher frequencies. Like the mirror, she will push you here and there. She will remind you of what you are here to do, and/or what you are here to change about yourself or your life. The teacher can be relentless, like the mirror, but she'll also be the most loving teacher you'll ever have. Besides, she will most likely be in the love frequencies herself while teaching you, and she can propel you into her frequency range, if you let her. The teacher is a great cat to have around, and you can always ask her to *teach* you how to increase your vibration!

♥ THE PROTECTOR

This one can be quite obvious in what he is doing, and you might not feel his love or joy frequencies as much as you do with other cats. However, this cat is *so* full of love for you that it'll shine through in everything that he does. For everything he ever does is protect you out of love and respect for who you are. So just revel in the protector's love frequencies, and appreciate and cherish that you are loved so much! It'll act as the proverbial tuning fork that we have cited so often now, and you'll automatically slip into the higher frequencies when you are around this cat – if or when you'll let the process happen consciously.

As we said before, it's all about consciously evoking your cat's magic, so you can knowingly move into and receive and then later *uphold* the frequencies of love and joy within you.

So let's round out our list with the two last archetypes:

♥ THE REBEL

You might find it challenging to find love and joy frequencies around him, for he can be very intense and serious at times. But underneath all his toughness, underneath that coat of armor that he shows on the outside, there is a very soft core and a very tender heart that beats for one person: for you! Remember that this cat will do anything and everything in his power to show you where you need to change something in your life, because of his huge, unwavering love for you. He loves you so much that he is willing to play the bad guy role for however long it takes, until you change what needs to be changed in your life, so you'll get on track with your soul plan. Talk about tough love! Similar to the protector, the rebel, underneath his toughness, is swimming in the love frequencies, and when you let him, he'll help you attune to the higher vibrations and become a more loving person in the process.

♥ THE STARSEED

Yay! We've arrived at our last archetype and this one, of course, is easy. She is already at a supercharged high frequency because that is her very nature. She is full of Ascension energies and she has an inbuilt high-vibe mode. So the longer you stay around her, the more she will "rub off" on you, and we don't mean just behavior-wise, but mainly frequency-wise. She will shift you naturally and effortlessly, from *I don't know what I'm doing in this Ascension process* to *I am shifting day-by-day, week-by-week, month-by-month*. And in a year, you are a completely different person! The starseed cat is one of the easiest to help you shift your vibration and one of the easiest to help you stay in the higher realms. For once you *know* that you are a starseed and have a cosmic soul mission, there is no *un*-knowing it. There is no *un*-doing the changes and shifts that are happening in your consciousness and your beingness. So embrace your cat's magical ability to shift your vibration to the realms of love and joy, and be happy and grateful to have her in your life.

This was the list of cats' abilities to help you shift into the higher vibrations. And we want to add that just as with everything else: don't overthink it! *The cats are chuckling*, because they know that their beloved humans are now thinking about what they just read, and thinking of ways to do it, and the how's and the when's. And they are saying: just be yourself! We are by your side to help with the heavy lifting. *Your* job is to be *YOU*. To come into your true self. And *we* are helping with the *HOW*. So when you are in our company, think of the above. You know by now what archetype each of your cats is, and you can then take this book as a little guide, and we'll do the rest.

17

YOUR SACRED SOUL MISSION

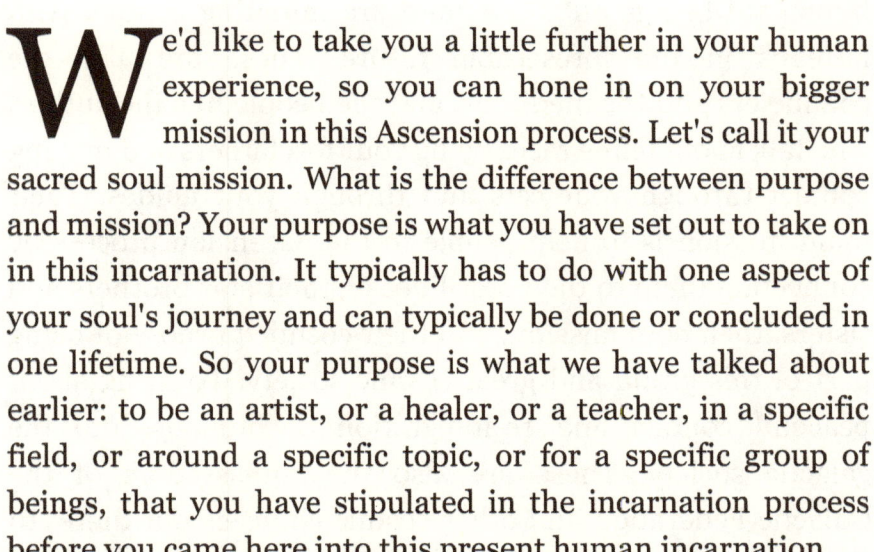

We'd like to take you a little further in your human experience, so you can hone in on your bigger mission in this Ascension process. Let's call it your sacred soul mission. What is the difference between purpose and mission? Your purpose is what you have set out to take on in this incarnation. It typically has to do with one aspect of your soul's journey and can typically be done or concluded in one lifetime. So your purpose is what we have talked about earlier: to be an artist, or a healer, or a teacher, in a specific field, or around a specific topic, or for a specific group of beings, that you have stipulated in the incarnation process before you came here into this present human incarnation.

Let's zoom out into the bigger picture now: your soul mission is bigger than that! Bigger than what any one person can achieve in one lifetime, and bigger than your human mind can usually wrap your head around, so to speak. The human missions are more of a divine nature, and they usually come in groups. Let's call it your soul group, for instance, and what your soul group or soul mission typically revolves around.

✦ THE STARSEED MISSION GROUP

Let's start with the obvious ones, the ones coming from the stars, here to bring enlightenment, peace, and expansion of your horizon as a cosmic being and a cosmic citizen. They are the ones that are assisting in what you call the disclosure process. The ones that bring the knowledge to humans that there are other civilizations, other lifeforms, in short: other humanoid beings out there, and are initiating contact with humans in the foreseeable future. These are also the channelers and the mediums, and the people like the author, who talk about feline races being your forefathers and making contact through your cats and through your guides. Their main mission is to help people in the Ascension process by connecting them to their star lineage, their star brothers and sisters, their soul mission, and their cosmic purpose of being part of this grand and great cosmic society. To bring about peaceful contact and re-integration of humans into the galactic society. These are also the ambassadors of the Galactic Federation and other cosmic counsels out there. In short, this soul mission group is here to reunite humans with their galactic origins and their starseed origins.

As we already explained, all humans are technically star-related, with many star nations having put their DNA into them. So *all* humans that are on this planet or that have chosen to go through the Ascension process and that are still here at this point in time will be awakened to their galactic origins. And there are some that will depart and choose to *not* be part of this disclosure, and that is okay. Most of the ones that are still here will move on.

✨ THE GALACTIC PLANNERS

This group are the ones that are actually out there overseeing planets, the land masses, the oceans. They are the ones actively working with stargates and planetary systems. So this is the task of those who feel drawn to gridwork and working with the oceans, the land, the ancient ley lines, etc., in this incarnation on Earth. These are also the ones that delve deep into astrology and astronomy. They might not be aware of their "bigger" task and that they are actually out there in their astral bodies doing this kind of work on a much larger scale than they know. How do they do it? Simply by connecting to the stars, the land masses, the oceans, the waters, the ley lines of the Universe, the planetary bodies, systems, stargates, etc. Those who are in this line of work will typically know at this point *"this is me"*.

So these soul group missions are something you'll do over a long period of time, even before you came here. You've been doing this forever and your Earthly purpose is usually in line with it.

✧ THE SOUL LIGHT GUARDIANS

This group are the ones with the light warrior tasks here on Earth but on a bigger scale. These guardians are both powerful and fierce, but also full of light. They are the ones you see with hoodies in the astral realm, they are the ones you see as guardian angels, and yes, some of the archangels might fall into that category. If you are of the guardian soul group, then you'll know it. You are here to protect, to oversee, to help out anyone in need, and to keep whole planets and nations safe. They oversee the population movements from one planet to another. They oversee when a planet goes through a period of change, and people/beings need rescuing or rehoming. They are actually here right now, bringing those humans that chose to stay in 3D to other planetary systems, meaning their souls are being helped to go to another place where they can continue their soul's journey in more 3D incarnations before they are ready to move up and beyond.

So this is your soul group assignment. There are others, of course, but these three are the main groups in which you typically participate in this bigger scheme of soul evolution and expansion of consciousness. You will usually know if you are a **guardian**, or a **planner (gridworker)**, or an **ambassador for the star nations.**

Now let's get into how this is important and ties into everything that we are teaching in this book. The cats are part of this grander game, and yes, their souls are part of these soul incarnations as well. There are guardians (dogs fall into this category), there are ambassadors (cats typically) and there are also planners among the animals.

But let's stick to the human soul missions a little longer. So while your life purpose is something that you can easily achieve in one lifetime, your soul mission is something bigger, grander, and spans over many many many lifetimes and over the course of millennia, or sometimes longer. There are some readers here who are even older and come from a different universal expression, and you'll know if you have a knowledge beyond this. But most people will know that they are here to do one of these three main tasks. They are the building blocks of this Universe: to build, to guard, to expand and bring together.

So you as a human being in this grander scheme can now step up to your task and truly embrace who you are. Say you are a starseed ambassador; you could just choose to go and do your "smaller" tasks from this lifetime, or you can go beyond and reach further into your "true" and bigger task. Why would you do that? So you can expand beyond your human horizon and become bigger than life in this lifetime! And this is truly needed in this Ascension process, that people wake up to their super-humanness, to their abilities beyond abilities.

How do you do that? Simple. Just feel in... Which soul group are you? And once you know: How can you serve in this bigger mission? What can you contribute?

There are some who are already doing it and others who still need some awakening. We want to awaken you today, right here, and right now, to your soul mission groupness and to your sleeping beautyness, and to how you can now wake up and be truly *YOU*!

18

YOUR CAT'S HIGHER SOUL MISSION

As we established earlier, cats are the tuning forks for their human's vibration. They are so inherently entwined with their human companions, that they are doing this tuning incessantly, all the time, and by their very nature.

The humans are usually very much entwined with their cats as well and with their soul contracts. Let's talk about soul contracts for a moment. We already touched on the fact that you, before you incarnate into a new life here on Earth, make all these soul contracts with other beings. With the humans you'll meet during your lifetime, and with your animal companions. So the cats really do sign up to be with you. They do so voluntarily and fully committed to their jobs.

Your cat is helping you happily and voluntarily

We'd like to mention this to all those humans who say they don't want their cats to suffer physically, or emotionally, or take on their human's "stuff". Know that your cat does this happily, readily, voluntarily, and so to speak by divine decree because you both agreed to being travel buddies during your incarnations. Just like you signed up to do what you are currently here to do, including all the hardships and all the tough jobs and karmic imprints and core wounds you agreed to clear for humanity during your stay here, so did your cat!

So please don't get too distraught over your cat taking on your issues, or even more importantly, don't try to take your cat's job (for instance, to help you carry your emotional baggage) away from them. Just like you would not enjoy sitting on your behind your entire life and doing nothing but eat and sleep and knit and watch TV... neither does your cat! The ups and downs in life, the good with the bad, is what makes living so juicy and so interesting on this planet. So don't tell your cat to stay out of your business, or to not take on your "stuff"... because she does what she needs to do, and what she is here to do.

The soul contracts between you and your cat are usually manyfold and can be quite complicated at times. But they can also be straightforward and simple: to be there for each other in love and respect, to help each others' journey progress and thrive, and to work towards a common goal.

It is important for us to stress this part because we cats hear it quite often that you don't want us to take on our human's issues. But know that no matter how hard it looks for you what we do, it comes effortlessly and easily to us, and it is usually an integral part of our being.

You can help your cat by helping yourself

How can you help your cat then, if you feel she might take on too much from you? Well, by working on overcoming your emotional topics and heavy "stuff" yourself and moving into the higher frequencies. Then your cat can let go of the "stuff" she helps you carry, and you'll both be a step further in the right direction.

So let's summarize the cats' part in humanity's soul process. We are closely entwined with you on a soul level. We come here with our special purr-poses and soul missions. We accompany you through whatever part of your life you need us for, and sometimes lifetime after lifetime. And we'd like to conclude this portion of the book by saying how great and proud we are to be of service to humans. And how we lovingly watch over you on your path. And how we cats are active parts of your Ascension journey. And that now you have everything you need to go forward in love and joy.

19

LIVING IN LOVE AND JOY

T he cats want to add a final chapter, to round out this collection of knowledge. And the final chapter is all about *LOVE* and finding that same *LOVE* for yourself that you have for your cats. To start off the book, the cats talked about themselves, and about their purr-pose. Then that led into *YOUR* purpose and your soul contracts here on Earth and for the Ascension process. This led into the New You and the True You chapter, in which the cats were leading the way, so you can understand that by being in the higher frequencies of joy and love, you can create the great life that you are here to live. For you are the ultimate creator of your experience, and your cats are here to help you be all that you can be. So in this context, we showed you that your mission is to be you. And to create. And to bring this Earth project to fruition. Thus the icing on the cake is to elevate yourself into the state of pure, unconditional love. And this state is the pinnacle. We are leading you from *JOY,* which is easier to accomplish and practice, into the state of *LOVE* and then *BLISS*. Let's elaborate.

We cats, to reiterate this very important point, are here to help elevate the frequency of this planet to the state of 5D, the New Earth, the experience of love and joy in a physical body. That is the state that many beings in the greater universal experience are in while in a physical body. Both Earth and humanity are on their way to that state of being, of existence. However, the cats are mostly already there! That is one of our cat secrets: we already live in a state of joy and unconditional love.

Cats are masters in being themselves

How does this play out, or how do we experience this? Just by being ourselves and not pretending to be something or someone else. By appreciating life and everything it offers, to the fullest. By being in a state of bliss when we are savoring the moment. When we are lying in the grass and enjoying the moment. Hearing the birds. Watching our favorite humans go about their business and their daily routine. Eating and enjoying our food. Being in a state of relaxation and gratitude and eternal understanding that everything is as it is for a reason. Yes, even if our life is not perfect at this point in time, we'll still find a reason to be grateful for what we have and that we are even here.

So the joy is one thing... the pure joy of living that we usually have, when we are in our unadulterated state of being a cat, when we live with humans and share your human lives. Let's mention again at this point that, yes, some cats will take on their human's emotional baggage, and can get into a state of anxiety or stress. But at the same time, and this is important, they never forget that this is a *state* they are in, while deep inside knowing that it is not *them*, that it is not their natural state of being. The difference for humans is that you'll identify yourself with that anxious state of being. You identify yourself with that fear, that feeling of unworthiness, that disdain for your body or your looks, and that feeling of not being at ease with your life.

For us cats, it's a bit different. Yes, we can have all the dense feelings and heavy emotional states you have, and yes, we come with our own issues and challenges and life topics. But deep inside we won't let it define us! We usually have a good sense of it being just a facade, just a role we're playing, and that we are truly here in service and in joy and in love for who we are and the role we are playing here. So in that sense, we cats are more in the understanding that we *are* divine. That we *are* part of god. That we *are* love. And that is how we can uplift and inspire you to get to that same state. If you'll let us help you get there or let us get in the lead.

Cats spend their days in natural flow

The cats are here to help you get into a similar state of pure love. Of knowing who you are and how you can express yourself or your divine self fully in this body. How do the cats do it? By simply following their heart and following their unique expression of who they are. How does this play out on a daily basis? Well, a cat will get up and do her grooming. Her eating. Her going outside. Her sharpening her claws. Her climbing and getting some exercise. And then, she will spend time with her human when she feels like it or when her human is in need of her company. In short, she'll spend her day in "flow", as her higher self is guiding her.

You, as humans, are of course driven or guided by your human rules and the schedules that you have made up for yourselves as a society. We cats do understand that there are guidelines you are following. Your designated sleeping schedule (while we cats sleep when we're tired or when our body tells us to rest). Your personal eating schedules: the when's, the what's, the how's, and all the conditioning that comes with it. Your work schedule. Your free time schedule. Yes, you humans even put a schedule behind your "free" time!

We are not saying that to make fun of you. We merely want to point out that with all your scheduling, you put yourself in a box of very limited time of just pure beingness. So what do we suggest you do? Well, we understand you cannot just break away completely from your schedule and human society rules.

But we do recommend you take time to breathe every once in a while... and maybe loosen your schedule a little bit. The parts that you *do* have control over, your "free time", for instance. Don't press yourself into a schedule in your free time. If you feel like reading, then read. If you feel like going for a walk, then do that. If you feel like doing nothing and just looking out over your yard, sitting there with a cup of coffee, and doing nothing... then by all means, do that! Listen to your body more: does your body want to move or does it need rest? Does your body really want to eat? Or is your eating hour a habit drilled into your subconscious?

When you start the practice of really, truly listening to your body and what you *really* want at any point in time, then you'll be one step further to where you want to be: in your body, in this lifetime, on your way to enlightenment, and creating your dream life in this existence. And remember, your dream life does not always have to involve winning the lottery, but your dream life has everything to do with you being the highest expression of yourself. As a creator. As a divine being living in love and joy. As a lover, a joybringer, an artist, a healer, and so on. Add your creator archetype here, and imagine living your life as the highest expression of this. Not in anxiety and stress and dutifulness, but in the highest expression of loving what you do, and doing what you love.

Take your cat as your guide

This is where we are leading you in this chapter. Take your cat as your example, and live more in the flow of life. Once you manage to spend your days more and more in *JOY* (or once you *EN-JOY* your day more and more), you'll be moving into the highest soul expression of you. And once you embody more and more what you *LOVE* being or doing (an artist, a healer, a scholar, an ambassador...), then you'll get more and more into the *LOVE* frequencies. Which is where you want to be most of your time. Not necessarily right now, not yet. You can, but don't stress yourself out if you are not. Remember, this is a journey, not an arrival at a destination within three days. Instead, train yourself to be more and more in the *EN-JOY* mode during your day. Take the little breaks in between, and listen to your body and your emotions more. And move more towards your *PURPOSE* and your creation archetype, and you'll add more of that into your day. And then, after a while, after practicing the *EN-JOY YOUR DAY* mode more and more, you'll automatically slip into the *I LOVE MY LIFE* mode, and you'll become more and more the *TRUE YOU*.

This is what the cats wanted to share in this last chapter of summing up their teachings, and rounding out how they help you get into your divine mission and divine purpose creator mode.

How else can they help you? Well, the way they do it every day: by *DOING* their wonderful jobs with you, and at the same time by *BEING* their wonderful selves... thereby leading by example and inspiring you to do or be the same. And lastly, by being in the natural joy and love frequencies themselves, and thereby attuning you to it (tuning fork principle), and thereby enriching the human field and the entire Earth experience with these frequencies.

So we cats truly are here to bring LOVE and JOY to this experience and to humanity. We are truly honored that we were part of this channeling experience, and we are not phasing out this book.

May this be your gift to present to the world: who we truly are as cats, as a species, how we are related to humans, and how we came to be here. And how we continue to serve and love humanity and help co-create this experience and this New Earth, together with humanity and all the other wonderful beings and star nations and light beings that are helping in this experience.

It has truly been an honor. We love you, we love you, we love you.

 **THE CATS**

20

Q&A WITH THE CATS

———— 🐾 ————

After I came out of the channeling mode, I as the author of this book had a few more questions about the concepts shared by the cats and the Collective. So in the spirit of tying up loose ends and clarifying some of the metaphysical concepts for the readers, here is my follow-up Q&A with the cats and my higher guidance.

About the joy frequencies

Q: Can you please elaborate a bit more about the joy frequencies?

This is the state you are in when you are in deep gratitude for the world you live in. The book you are reading. The cat you are cuddling with. The water you are swimming in. The food that you are cooking. The friend you are talking to. The nature you see and experience around you. The night sky you are looking at. Or the car you are happily driving, enjoying its feel and speed. Basically, the action you are consciously doing while being in alignment with it and with who you truly are.

Everything and anything you *en-joy* doing and reveling in is what brings you into the joy frequencies. It's about taking pleasure in the beauty and the simplicity of life, enjoying it with all your senses, just like the cats do: the tactile experience, the scents, the visuals, the sounds, the energies that you *feel* and perceive through your body and your existence.

Q: How can we get there more frequently or more permanently?

We cats would say it is really easy: include more things in your day that give you joy, rather than doing a lot of things that you resist or don't like doing. Just for starters, include at least 2 things in your day that *truly* give you joy. Like playing with your cat for a few minutes a day. Or going for a walk, or whatever you *en-joy* doing. Then stretch that time a bit, by say, including 3 things or 5 things per day in it. But don't force it. Let it happen naturally, and before you know it, you'll have more *JOY* in your overall life experience, and you'll live more and more in the *JOY* frequencies.

Q: What about those people who feel they are not worthy of a truly great life?

Well, let's see it from our cat perspective. Why would you, the marvel and crown jewel of creation, not be worthy of living in love and joy? You are the creator of this world! You, in your complexity of the human race, are the creators of your own experience! So from our cat perspective, why would the creator not enjoy his daily creations? Why would *YOU*, the center of *YOUR* life, of your Universe, of your daily experience, create something that you are *NOT* worthy of?

Q: Can you help us get over that?

Gladly, and we cats do that in all the ways we described in the channeling. Yes, not all humans are on the same level of joy, and some have more hardships to go through than others. We get that. But not all of your experience has to be about you not being able to *ENJOY* yourself.

Q: How can we be joyful when so many others are suffering?

We understand there is still much hardship going on in the world. But that makes the conjuring of joy even more important: to shift the overall planetary frequency, and especially the human field to a higher vibratory state! The more people shift into the joy frequencies, the more you'll elevate and uplift all of humanity.

Know that joy doesn't come at the expense of others when it truly comes from the heart. And that's what your cat helps you with day in and day out: stay in your heart in everything you say, do, or think. Be the person you are when you hold your cat, when you cuddle with your cat, when you stroke your cat's soft fur. At that moment, you are in your truest, highest joy frequency, and this is the feeling, the *YOU* that we want you to portray to the world.

About the love frequencies

Q: Can you please elaborate a bit more on the love frequencies?

Sure, the cats would love to explain the love frequencies. As we shared earlier, it is the highest frequency out there, the god frequency, if you will.

We understand that the joy frequencies are easier to access for our humans. They are on the spectrum just below the love frequency. It is easier, from your human perspective, to add activities to your day that will give you that feeling of fun, joy, contentment, and satisfaction. Easy: like eating your favorite food, or cuddling with your cat, or reading a good book. That puts you in the *JOY* frequencies for a while.

We realize that *LOVE* is not harder to achieve, but it is more about a state of *being* and not necessarily *doing*. So while you can always add an *action* to your day (see above) to get to that enjoyment state... the love frequencies are more about a *mindset*, a way of being.

Let's elaborate. The love frequencies are something you are truly inherently born with – we all are. We come into this life completely unaware of what's in store for us. Unaware that there might be anything not loving or not peaceful in this world. For where we came from, where our soul was before reincarnating, we were in a state of peace and happiness and unity and just beingness.

Then we come into a physical body and *WOW*, this experience here is taking us for a ride! So we take on all kinds of distortions, wounds, beliefs, etc. Most of these we take on ourselves or make up about ourselves, and much of it has to do with the mother wound or the mother imprint that we are getting at birth. When our mother seemingly doesn't love us enough, it leaves an imprint: that we are not loveable. Or when our mother doesn't love or value herself, that is a similar imprint: that we are also not loveable enough or that we need to perpetuate our mother's imprint. And so on.

So the mother wound of our present incarnation is what induces us into a state of not being our full selves or not loving ourselves the way we truly are when we are whole and complete, un-incarnated, and in our purest soul form. But self-love is the basic building block for reaching unity consciousness and for loving others!

Q: How can we get more into the love frequencies?

The love frequencies are reachable when we get into a state of oneness with who we are, what our role and archetype is, and finding our *True You* state. So follow the steps with the golden spark of Source consciousness that you come from. Then follow up on "who you are" on the spectrum of your role here (your creator/purpose archetype) and your soul essence (your soul mission group) that is your highest expression. Follow the *True You* chapter, and it will lead you right to *YOU*.

And then, when you are in your *YOU* state, you'll fully embrace the love frequencies. Having love for yourself, and for everything and anyone out there. For the *LOVE* frequencies are the state of love and joy and oneness that you are here to achieve, and to usher in the New Earth for yourself and your loved ones.

Being in the *LOVE* frequencies is the pinnacle of your existence. So in a sense, you won't get there overnight, but it is part of the journey this book takes you on, so that over time you can learn to live in love and joy.

Q: How do you describe the love frequencies?

The love frequencies are a state of being, where you are one with all of creation. Where you can see the "good" and the "bad" and not judge. Where you can be either in a non-corporeal state and be your true self in your soul or spirit form, or you can enjoy this state of being in your human and physical form, which is what you are here to achieve.

So don't be upset if you are not yet in a state of love frequency at all times. This is your journey that you are here to do, to achieve, to revel in. Once you have achieved a more permanent state of love frequencies, you are becoming who you truly are: a master of your experience.

About the Cat Secret

Q: So at the end of the day, what really is the cat secret?

Purpose. Love. Creation. Joy. Essentially, all of it. It is up to you to discern what you want to call the cat secret in this book.

Q: What do you feel is the biggest takeaway for the readers of this book?

That it is all about *BEING YOU*, about being your best self, about living in the love and joy frequencies, about being all that you can be, about embodying the *TRUE YOU*.

So the cat secret is really simple: the cats are showing you how to be the highest expression of yourself, while living in love, joy, and purr-pose.

Author: Thank you so much!

You are welcome. We love you, we love you, we love you. It was a pleasure doing this project with you. The cat collective, your cats Lennie, Lisa, Jamie, Leon, Sheila, Aaron, and all the other cats that are channeling this for you.

We leave you in joy and love.

HOW TO GO FROM HERE

I hope you enjoyed this adventure of looking into the feline soul, mind, and psyche, and getting first-hand knowledge from our beloved feline friends. While the information that came through the channeling was not new to me, even I as the author was surprised at the depths of universal wisdom the cats wanted to share in this book.

If these messages resonate with you, then I invite you to take this beautiful journey further. The content of this book is of a higher vibration and was giving you light codes and cosmic activations as you were reading it.

If you have gone through the steps laid out in this book, as in understanding your cat's archetype, embracing your life purpose and soul mission, discovering your galactic origins, becoming the New You, and moving towards the True You, then you are already on your way to living a life full of love, joy, and purr-pose.

Wherever you stand in this process, remember to always have your cat help you along the way! **Find out more at:**

www.sylviesterling.com

For starters: Listen to your cat

If you continue this journey by yourself, then I am wishing you lots of love, and many great moments of love, joy, and awakening together with your cat companion.

You can always go to my online academy for more resources and inspiration. **Feline Soul Academy is a magical place of transformation and awakening,** guided by the cats. You can find everything you need around cat communication, energy healing, spiritual and starseed awakening, and making a true soul connection with your cat at:

www.sylviesterling.com/academy

For curious souls: Embrace your mission

If you are serious about becoming the New You, finding your life purr-pose, and pursuing your soul mission, then I'd be happy to help you take the next steps.

You can find **guided meditations** to facilitate the processes described in this book, as well as **mini-classes, daily feline wisdom bits, and deepening of the Cat Secret teachings,** so you can enjoy your joint journey with your feline companion at:

www.sylviesterling.com/thecatsecret

For deep divers: Become a cosmic citizen

If you truly want to become a cosmic citizen, embody the True You, and embrace your galactic origins, then **let me introduce you to the Cat Secret Masterclass.**

I think you'll love this all-in transformational experience, so you can truly master living in love, joy, and purr-poseful creation while being the highest expression of yourself. Find out more about my Cat Secret Masterclass at:

www.sylviesterling.com/thecatsecret

Whatever you decide to do – go it alone or take up my invitation for guided meditations, classes, or deepening of the feline teachings – I wish you all the best on your Ascension journey. I know without a doubt that you have the best teacher and guide by your side that anyone can have: your cat companion.

Sending you love and purrs,

Sylvie & the Cats 🐾

ABOUT THE AUTHOR

Sylvie Sterling is an internationally acclaimed cat expert, cat whisperer, author, speaker, intuitive healer, spiritual teacher, Lyran starseed, Ascension guide, and channel of the Cat Collective. Passionate about being an ambassador for felines, Sylvie's mission is to forever change the way we see our beloved cat companions: not as cute little furballs, but as beautiful souls coming into our lives with the important task of guiding us on our soul path. Her work empowers cat lovers around the world to awaken to their true selves and their cosmic origins with the help of their cats. For more information and resources, please visit:

www.sylviesterling.com